UNSEEN LEADERSHIP

TALES OF UNSUSPECTING LEADERS

CODY J. COMSTOCK

ISBN 9798990232907 (ebook) | ISBN 9798990232914 (paperback) | ISBN 9798990232921 (hardcover)

1st Edition

This collection of leadership stories is dedicated to my wife, Kristen, and my three children, Cody Jr., KayLynn, and Jonah. May you all grow up to be the most impactful of leaders.

"THERE WILL ALWAYS BE SOMEONE
WHO CAN'T SEE YOUR WORTH. DONT
LET IT BE YOU." - MEL ROBBINS

CONTENTS

INTRODUCTION

In our intricate societal web of roles and responsibilities, we often frame leadership within the familiar narrative of power and authority. We conjure images of CEOs dictating corporate strategy, world leaders addressing nations, sports coaches tirelessly refining team dynamics, and university provosts setting educational standards. These individuals, with their sharp suits and charismatic speeches, are the obvious bearers of leadership in our society. Yet, beyond the polished surface of these obvious symbols, there lies a far more intricate world. Here, leadership takes on an entirely different form, subtly resounding in seemingly inconsequential acts of everyday life.

However, leadership—real, genuine transformational leadership—is more nuanced than these traditional snapshots. It is often the quieter corners of life where profound and transformative leadership unfolds, not within designated positions of authority, but within the rich context of everyday resilience, dedication, and creativity. These corners tell tales of leadership that resound with the symphony of human spirit, encapsulating the raw essence of our innate desire to inspire and be inspired.

Leadership, as we have come to discover, is more than just a virtue nestled within organizational charters or political mandates. It permeates through the fabric of our daily lives, revealing itself in acts of compassion, resiliency, and selflessness. Ordinary people, navigating the complexity of their existence, are capable of displaying extraordinary leadership in a myriad of circumstances.

This introduction merely scrapes the surface into the various ways individuals, irrespective of the traditional hallmarks of leadership, influence and create change in their environment—demonstrating that all walks of life are teeming with leaders, just waiting to be recognized and appreciated.

"Unseen Leadership" is an invitation for you to explore leadership in its truest sense—beyond formal titles and hierarchical structures. It removes the boundary conditions often associated with 'traditional leadership' and identifies leadership as an innate human phenomenon—a behavioral trait evident beyond the realms of corner offices, political arenas, or academic platforms. It is in the beating heart of a street performer, relentlessly chasing their passion amid adversity. It is in the crisp, unwavering voice of a protestor, advocating for justice with unyielding determination. It's even in the silent prayer of a humanitarian, stretching out a helping hand to those in need. We enter the corridors of hospitals, the quiet corners of libraries, the relentless machinery of factories, the warmth of households, and even the endearing chaos of classrooms.

As we embark on this journey, a question lingers—how can everyday people, perhaps like you and I, who don't inhabit defined leadership roles, exhibit leadership traits? Is it draped in the compassionate soul of a volunteer spending countless hours at a local shelter, making a difference one helpless creature at a time? Is it echoed in the disciplined commitment of a young athlete diligently training before dawn, inspiring those around with her dedication?

Or perhaps it's seen most clearly in the humble part-time worker, whose infectious enthusiasm and diligent customer service becomes the highlight of every customer's day. Take a moment to visualize the diligent, almost invisible worker, whose ingenuity and commitment to his mundane work leads to remarkable efficiencies within an organization. Or the empathetic teacher who subtly molds the minds of her students, guiding them into their futures and, unknowingly, leading a new generation towards responsible citizenship.

Our world brims with quiet heroes, showcasing unconventional leadership through subtle, yet profound ways. As we will discover, leadership is not just about authority; it's about inspiring change, driving progress, and building harmony, regardless of the platform or medium in which these qualities emerge.

You will encounter characters in this book who have mustered the strength and the courage to step up, not for the glare of public recognition or an expectation of appreciation, but because they felt an inherent sense of responsibility —they listened to the faint, yet unmistakable internal call to action. Their narratives brilliantly exemplify how leadership—making empathetic and farsighted decisions based on determination and inspiration—resides within each one of us, irrespective of our age, profession, or social status. On the other hand, you will also encounter characters whose leadership attributes are subtly present yet make the most surprising of impacts on those it reaches.

Take, for example, the introspective librarian who, propelled by her love for literature and a keen sense of social responsibility, assures the continuation of local education when the community schools are faced with devastating budget cuts. Her precise planning, flawless execution, and insurmountable drive to succeed single-handedly transformed the community's perception of altruism and leadership.

Visionaries like the graphic novelist who weaves heroic tales, embedding in the hearts and minds of young readers the value of courage and moral righteousness, teaching them to bravely question and challenge stifling norms. Or the compassionate nurse, placing a reassuring hand on a fearful patient's shoulder, using her calming presence to lead them through those dark moments of uncertainty towards hope.

Consider the infectiously vibrant barista, whose passion for coffee is only surpassed by his thirst for meaningful connections. This everyday philosopher, armed with a smile and an espresso machine, subtly steers regular customers towards an improved outlook on life and work, brewing up an atmosphere of positivity and companionship that goes beyond the confines of the café.

Step into the hallowed hallways of a nursing home, where an extraordinary caregiver weaves an atmosphere bustling with love, warmth, and cheer. Their ability to muster emotional strength during times of adversity, coupled with their unwavering dedication, transforms the mundane routine into a series of meaningful interactions, imbuing a seemingly ordinary job with extraordinary leadership.

Every story in this collection is a poignant reminder that leadership does not demand the grandeur of a podium, a captivated audience, or a glittering array of accolades. It is rooted in the contributions we make, the choices that adorn our character, the times we choose to stand tall in the face of adversity, and the instances where we dare to venture outside our comfort zones, all with the aim of benefiting not just ourselves, but the people and communities around us.

Moreover, leadership can be seen in day-to-day acts of kindness, the quiet gestures that reveal a person's generosity and compassion. Individuals who extend their time, resources, or emotional support for those grappling with life's challenges offer solace and hope to those fortunate enough to receive their attention. These unexpected heroes are the listeners, the comforters, and the protectors of the vulnerable and heartbroken —their empathy, emotional intelligence, and selflessness are all traits that elevate their everyday acts into a true embodiment of leadership.

Redefining leadership requires introspection—it asks the resonant question: how do you conceive and enact your influence? Does it facilitate growth or perpetuate stagnation? Leadership isn't a privilege confined to a select few, but an opportunity that is generously offered to all. You are a part of the symphony of life, and your every action and encounter is a chance to lead, inspire, and impact.

As you turn the pages of this book, I invite you to reflect on your manifestation of leadership, the potential for transformation that you carry within you, no matter where you stand in life. It's easy to forget that our influence can alter the course of someone's day, spark fresh ideas, nudge someone to question the status quo, or inspire them to muster the courage to take a daunting leap of faith. Leadership isn't just about the grand narrative; it's often about the journey—the decisions, interactions, and the persevering spirit that collectively chart your life's path, thereby impacting others in your wake.

Each individual we encounter finds leadership in the delicate mix of their actions and intentions, their responses to life's continual challenges, and how they bear their part in the collective story we all share. In recognizing this, we not only celebrate these silent leaders, but also, we realize the dormant leader within us, waiting for the right moment to emerge, influence, and inspire.

"Unseen Leadership" is so much more than just a collection of stories; it's a mirror reflecting your innate potential for leadership. It brings to fore the countless heroes around us who bravely step up to shape a brighter tomorrow, inspiring us to comprehend that real leadership takes shape when we seize the initiative to make a difference, however small and however quietly. You are reflected in these pages, as a testament to the fact that leadership arises from our actions, not our titles.

Lastly, as you continue reading and deriving inspiration from these stories of unconventional leadership, let their vividness and depth inspire you to acknowledge and appreciate the leaders in your life, but more importantly, to recognize the leader within you. Through introspection, self-awareness, and a dedication to making an impact — however small, however mundane — you, too, can emerge as a true leader, one day, one interaction, and one decision at a time. Leadership lives within all of us, and it's time we let it shine.

THE POWER OF AN UNSEEN LEADER

The term "Leadership"—a potent concept often evokes images of people exercising command, governing from positions of authority, exuding a tantalizing influence over many. While this conventional understanding of leadership is not misguided, it is regrettably constrained in its perspective. Leadership, in its most elemental and profound manifestation, should not merely be perceived as a privilege reserved for individuals perched high atop organizational or sociopolitical hierarchies. Instead, much like the tenacious roots that uphold a towering tree or the silent yet indispensable strands that constitute a rich, multilayered tapestry, impactful leadership often dwells unobserved beneath the surface before it bursts forth in the most unexpected and enriching of ways.

At its heart, leadership is embedded within the humility of service. It is underpinned by an unswerving drive to impact others positively and finds its home in the very essence of our shared human experiences. Leadership is not about a grand position, nor is it about being in the spotlight—it is about having the willingness and drive to serve, inspire others, and affect positive change. Leadership is about our humanity, our shared experiences, and our collective, coordinated endeavor.

Imagine strolling through the bustling, complex design of an urban city, or walking along the tranquil undulating path of a serene, picturesque country road. Envision how your journey intersects, crisscrosses, and forms a meshwork with the myriad of journeys of the countless people you pass by. Each individual you encounter carries with them a tapestry abundantly woven from their unique and diverse life experiences. These human canvases, each masterfully painted with extraordinary moments, often encompass acts of leadership that have laid the foundation for lasting impacts on the lives of others—more often than not, these acts go unnoticed even by the individuals who committed them.

To uplift these buried threads into visibility, let's breathe life into some of these stories. Picture a middle-aged man marking the end of his career life, bidding farewell before stepping into the realm of retirement. His unwavering integrity and deeply ingrained work ethic, though frequently underappreciated, have served as subtle influencing forces on his colleagues. Or perhaps, consider a young, energetic student venturing overseas to volunteer her time and effort to the needs of total strangers in a remote land. The depth of her compassion ignites an enduring flame in the hearts of those living in poverty, thereby potentially changing the course of their lives.

Reflect on an elderly retired individual who, devoid of any personal gain, devotes countless hours at a public library reading to young, impressionable children. His service unknowingly sparks a lifelong love for literacy and learning in the minds of the young ones who are the future of our society. Then, think of a young woman providing her undivided attention and a listening ear to a friend's struggles. This lets her friend tap into her resilience and skillfully navigate the tumultuous seas of her trials.

These unsung heroes may not don the mantle of leaders in the traditional sense. Yet, through their committed dedication to aiding others, often without conscious recognition or reward, they are indeed leaders making their mark at the grassroots level—the heart of societal fabric. Each person in this anthology of life brings with them a subtle yet potent form of leadership—the capacity to see beyond their immediate sphere, to go beyond what is expected of them, and to seize elusive opportunities that enable them to shape someone else's life positively.

An earnest desire to serve without any expectation of a quid pro quo or public acknowledgment sows the seeds of true leadership. It is a yearning embedded in our very human nature that seeks to express itself, to sprout amidst our daily lives. Its growth is not dictated by external recognition or favor but fueled by the humble satisfaction of serving others and contributing to the larger good.

Through these unpretentious engagements, these individuals ignite a chain reaction of inspiration and motivation. Each act of kindness, each gesture of compassion or empathy, each encouraging word and every smile inspires others and opens avenues for them to emulate similar qualities. This domino effect spreads outwards from its source in ever-expanding circles, much like radio waves rippling out from their epicenter. It fosters the growth of shared goodness like a nurturing sunshine, strengthens people's connections like a sturdy bridge, and augments our collective humanity, knitting together the diverse fabric of society.

In the journey of evolving into a more

effective, impactful leader, it is essential to foster a heightened, acute sense of awareness. This awareness is about recognizing the ripple effects our words, attitudes, and actions can have within our social environment. We need to proactively acknowledge our potential capacity to influence, stimulate, and induce change, as these abilities considerably shape the broader social fabric of which we are a part.

Recognizing such potential within us empowers us to empower others. It allows us to create space for them to share their journeys in their unique ways and to support them in delineating their individual paths, imbued with their strength and resilience. Empathy is at the marrow of this process. By aligning our feelings with someone else's experiences, be it their joy or struggle, their hopes, or their inexplicable pain, we become more effective in providing the support they need.

An outstretched hand of assistance, enveloped in understanding and acceptance, can not only guide another but can act as the catalyst needed to unleash the dormant potential within them. The awe-inspiring beauty of this process lies in its ripple effect—the modification of one thread has the potency to impact the others surrounding it, leading to an overall enrichment of the collective human experience.

Effectively influencing others through our daily

interactions engenders a profound and deeper sense of purpose, that goes beyond material gains. It lends us the ability to functionally craft our lives in a way that reflects our core human values of compassion and empathy. Such interactions invariably blur the dividing lines that separate the 'me' from 'us'. They foster a shared understanding, a solid interconnectedness, and a common endeavor towards establishing a more compassionate society.

Like a pebble cast into a still pond, our interactions—both intentional and unintentional—can generate waves of compassion that ripple out, reaching out earnestly to those near and far. These ripples of kindness, empathy, and understanding serve to bridge gaps, heal wounds, and inspire hope, thereby linking hearts in the most profound and unassuming ways and strengthening the collective human spirit.

As you engage more deeply in this exploration of everyday leadership—this journey of discovery and recognition—realize that with every thread you pull, every story you unravel, you are unearthing a rich illustration of humanity. These illustrations are brimming with experiences, emotions, trials, tribulations, victories, and wisdom. Every word you read, every insight you gain, each moment of reflection urges and inspires you to dive deeper into the sea of human experiences and connections.

Through these narratives and shared experiences, you are encouraged to advance in your journey to become a more compassionate, enlightened, and effect-oriented leader—one who appreciates the significant role and impact of small changes, subtle nudges, and patient listening. It encourages you to make a conscious effort to step beyond the restrictions of self-centered objectives, to shift the focus from 'me' to 'us.' It motivates you to upraise your mission towards a more benevolent one—one that constantly prompts, "How can I positively impact the lives of others, today and every day?"

As you dive deeper into this exploration, remember that leadership doesn't demand flashy actions or thunderous declarations—not always. Leadership, in essence, is about the will to serve, the courage to empathize, and the ability to inspire —and it reveals itself in the most unobtrusive way. It makes its presence felt amid the smallest acts of kindness, the simplest words of encouragement, and the silent gestures of support—all elements that bind us together in a web of empathy and shared responsibility.

Our individual threads of experiences, when woven together through shared experiences and aspirations, create an intricate, diverse picture of leadership—a shared narrative that beautifully captures the boundless potential of everyday people exercising considerable influence, shaping circumstances, and leaving indelible imprints in the hearts and lives of those they touch.

Embracing the idea that our everyday actions, insignificantly ordinary or seemingly trivial as they may seem, can have a far-reaching impact on the lives of others, brings into focus a larger picture. It ultimately makes us realize our shared existence, our interconnectedness, and our shared role in the concert of life. Upon recognizing our potential ripple effects, we become more compassionate, more empathetic, and more service-oriented—all genuine hallmarks of profound and impactful leadership. We unwittingly develop traits that can create remarkably positive change in the world, for such acts of compassion and empathy ripple out into the world, touching hearts and transforming lives.

Reflect on the numerous moments of your life when your unintended actions might have sparked a change, ignited a hope, or provided encouragement in ways you weren't even aware of. Let that sink in: the realization of how you and your actions—the seemingly insignificant choices you made—might have left an impact deep and wide. Let it inspire you to keep fueling this vast ripple effect through several more acts of everyday leadership—acts that resonate and radiate love and kindness. Each small act, each kind word, each smile has the potential to comfort, console, and encourage.

In the grand canvas of life, each story—no matter how small or seemingly inconsequential— is unique, valuable, and crucial. Your story, with all its shades, could potentially be a beacon of light guiding another's path. It could be the spark turbocharging the unwavering resolve of another individual, kindling their enthusiasm, and fueling their pursuit of excellence. Embrace this, treasure it, and do not underestimate the ripple effects that can emanate from it—impacts that can illuminate the world in profound and impressive ways.

Unraveling the concept of everyday leadership, we are frequently reminded that leadership is not a lofty concept meant solely for boardrooms, classrooms, or political campaigns. It exists in every corner of our world—in homes, schools, bakeries, and malls, on playgrounds, and along walking trails. Leadership lives within each act of kindness, in every instance of patient listening, amidst quiet acts of mutual assistance, and in spaces where love and respect flourish.

Through service, empathy, influence, and the simple act of being human, everyday leadership resounds in life's diverse events, subtly shaping a society more attuned to shared responsibilities, empathy, and compassion. Understanding this influence and recognizing the potential ripple effect that we can have on others, we can aspire to become more effective leaders—leaders who inspire and guide, leaders who nurture and build, leaders who leave irrefutable marks on the sands of time, wherever they set foot—influencing others, igniting change, and creating a significant impact in our daily lives.

THE QUIET INFLUENCER

In a small, serene town known as Picnic, nestled amidst hills and dales, there existed an institution whose venerable walls bore witness to generations of dreams and aspirations. This esteemed establishment was the Picnic Primary School - a building that, despite the ravages of time, stood tall as an embodiment of community spirit, an enduring reservoir of memories. Amidst the many classrooms and bustling corridors of Picnic Primary School, there lay the school library, acting as the heart of the esteemed institution.

The library, this wondrous space of silence, wisdom, and imagination, was a cornerstone of the small community's educational foundation and a nurturing haven for young minds who traversed on journey after magical journey through compelling stories that filled its shelves. The library served as a sanctuary for the students, where one could escape the ongoing struggles of formal education and fall into the comforting arms of a beautiful story.

One fateful day, however, like a sudden, unanticipated storm, a distressing announcement reverberated through the halls of Picnic. The school board had pronounced an unsettling decision - owing to crippling budget cuts, the once cherished and revered library was fated to shut its doors permanently. As the dark clouds of the news enveloped the entire town, it cast a deep despair and sorrow among the inhabitants. Like saplings robbed of their sunlight, the children and families of Picnic felt the chilly touch of bleakness on their future, with their once-vibrant, knowledge-rich sanctuary poised on the precipice of oblivion.

Amid the monoliths of stories and appellations of the Picnic Library, a quiet introverted soul named Louise sat wreathed within a cocoon of dust and forgotten leather-bound tomes. A modest librarian with an affinity for the literary world, Louise had spent many years roaming these very aisles and searching for solace and companionship among rows of familiar friends in the form of books. Thus, upon hearing the dispiriting news, sorrow and trepidation overcame her, and she mourned the imminent closure of a refuge that had shaped the intellectual landscape of her own and countless young minds before them.

It was a sunny morning when Louise found

herself standing outside the office of Tom Williams, a stern-faced city official who held unwavering faith in the decisions made by the school board. With her heart pounding in her chest, she knocked on the door and timidly entered, clutching a folder that contained all her proposals and calculations.

"Mr. Williams," she began cautiously, "I am Louise, the librarian at Picnic Primary School. I have come to discuss the recent decision to shut down the school library due to budget constraints."

Unmoved, Tom leaned back in his chair and adjusted his glasses. "Ah yes, Louise. I'm aware of the circumstances. Unfortunately, the school board was left with no other option. Tough decisions had to be made, and sacrifices must be accepted."

Fighting against the urge to retreat, Louise wiped her sweaty palms on her skirt and pressed on. "I disagree, Mr. Williams, and here's why," she explained, unveiling her carefully thought-out strategy and her plans to raise funds for the library. Her voice wobbled at first but quickly gained momentum as she passionately spoke of the library's significance to their town's future generations.

Tom   reluctantly   browsed   through   her

documents, barely concealing his impatience. "Louise, I appreciate your passion, but I assure you we've considered every option. The library had to go. We have to be practical."

Once Louise left Mr. William's office, she pondered the irreplaceable loss that awaited the school community. Destiny stirred within her a quiet, steely resolve - an urgent and powerful sense of obligation to save the storied sanctum of Picnic that had nursed so many young dreams, including her own. Driven by this silent determination, the introverted librarian stepped outside the comfortable boundaries of her inner sanctuary and embarked upon the herculean task of forging a neighborhood book drive. Although this enormous task appeared insurmountable, Louise possessed an unwavering belief in the library's importance to their town's future generations and education as a whole.

Embracing the challenge with inevitable doubts, Louise formulated an intricate plan that employed her services to set a brave and purposeful wheel into motion. Every day, as her tasks at the library reached their end, Louise would traverse the town's alleys and sidewalks, visiting homes, shops, and local gathering places to rally the residents around the desperate, yet much-needed, cause of saving the school library.

Summoning her inexhaustible patience and

meticulous attention to detail, Louise broke down the enormous undertaking into digestible tasks, delegating responsibilities with a delicate yet formidable touch that only an introvert could offer. Beginning with her close connections among friends, acquaintances, and fellow librarians, they meticulously planted the seeds of what they would come to know as a literary revolution - the restoration of the Picnic Primary School library.

One sunny afternoon, fate steered Louise's path towards the residence of an elderly woman named Mrs. Johnson, a former student of Picnic Primary School.

As Louise shared her plans and aspirations, Mrs. Johnson listened attentively, her eyes glistening with tears. Upon hearing Louise's dedicated pitch, she clasped the librarian's hands tightly and whispered, "Louise, I thank you from the bottom of my heart. It warms my soul to see someone so dedicated to preserving the legacy and knowledge held within our beloved library. I grew up with those books, and it brings me joy to see them cherished once more."

Touched by the sincere gratitude in Mrs. Johnson's voice, Louise felt her resolve solidify, revitalizing her commitment to save the library. "Thank you, Mrs. Johnson," she responded earnestly, "Your kind words mean more to me than words can describe. I won't relent until our library is restored to its former glory."

Louise, wielding her inherent gift of a quiet and magnetic charm, first enlisted the support of select members of the community - chiefly, fellow introverted, book-loving souls who shared the characteristic qualities that defined Louise herself. Together, they sat in dim cafes and living rooms, strategizing over cups of tea and cinnamon-filled treats, charting out a meticulously mapped course to ensure their ambitious goal.

As the weeks developed, Louise devised inspired and resourceful methods to approach their mission, which ensured garnering public sentiment and building a foundation of support for the young campaign. Utilizing local media, social networks, and their extensive knowledge of literature to provide recommendations to revive the school library, Louise's influence began to spread throughout the town. Slowly, but steadily, Picnic's residents took note of the librarian's quiet determination and selfless dedication to the cause.

As the weeks turned into months, the initially hesitant community underwent a heartening transformation. What had begun as a reluctant rallying of the townspeople gradually evolved into an avalanche of collective action, with people from all walks of life and of all ages joining in the crusade to save the library. Individuals

- storekeepers, mothers, fathers, and children - began to share their favorite stories, contributing books, resources, and helping hands to the cause with eager enthusiasm.

The sense of shared commitment, the infectious spark ignited by the shy librarian had spread far and wide, breathing new life into the community even as it had done with the books they sought to save. What began as Louise's personal mission had evolved into a town-wide mission - one that burned bright with the hopes and dreams of generations past and future. As the residents converged in their support of the library, a beautiful unity forged organically from Louise's seemingly unassuming efforts.

In time, the school library's doors reopened - now bursting with more books, more stories, and more whispers of adventure than ever before. It would serve as a testament to Louise's ceaseless dedication to the power of stories that had shaped Picnic's destiny. Students lined up, wide-eyed with anticipation, sensing the power of the tales that waited within, promising to be the wellspring of knowledge and memories that quenched their yearning minds.

The once quiet librarian had become a symbol of hope and inspiration, teaching the people of Picnic that leadership does not necessitate vocal declarations or grand displays but resides in the everyday decisions made with determination, passion, and quiet humility. Louise had successfully directed the town through a storm with the power of her introverted spirit, and in doing so, showcased the wonders that could emerge from the depths of quiet, resilient souls.

As the children of Picnic Primary School raced down the hallways, brushing past the aisles of newly shelved books, a sense of warm hope and accomplishment infused the school atmosphere, uplifting the hearts of all who bore witness to its resurrection. For deep within each page, each ink-stained line that traced the contours of so many lives, lay the story of an unassuming librarian named Louise. This quiet hero demonstrated to their beloved town, and the generations of the literary world that leadership could manifest itself in the humblest of forms - the love for literature, the persistence of purpose, and the quiet drive to create a positive change in the world.

And so, as the sun set on a new chapter in the collective narrative of Picnic, Louise retired to her familiar seat among the stacks of books in the library, contemplating the odyssey that had grown from her love and respect for the written word. This legacy would live on, inspiring countless lives in Picnic to explore the power of stories and, in doing so, to discover within themselves the potential to be leaders driven by determination, humility, and undeterred resolve.

THE QUIET INFLUENCER | 27

For in each quiet leader like Louise, there lays an emblem of growth, change, and deep-rooted human connections. A spark carried and vaulted with every turn of a page, igniting within each heart the indomitable power of stories, dreams, and journeys yet untold.

The Whisper of The Quiet Influencer

In this same quaint, hilly town of Picnic, where time seemed to linger and life felt unhurried, resided a young boy named Charlie. A resident of Picnic since birth, Charlie had often found himself nestled amidst the riches of the library, within the stories and worlds that presented themselves in the papery preserves of the town's cherished institution - the Picnic Library. This sanctuary of knowledge had been the source of Charlie's solace and inspiration, largely due to the gentle, introverted librarian Louise. Louise's quiet leadership had not only achieved the resurgence of Picnic's beloved library but had also left an indelible imprint on the hearts of Picnicians, especially young Charlie.

Louise's resilience and determination had been the beacon that lit the path for countless young minds, including Charlie. Her love for literature had transcended the confines of the library, extending into the lives of the townspeople and inspiring them to value the power of stories and collective action. From Louise's quiet leadership,

Charlie had gleaned something profound - that leadership was not about grand gestures or loud proclamations, but about compassion, perseverance, and the quiet determination to make a difference.

Having watched Louise closely, Charlie admired the soft-spoken librarian - not for her verbal eloquence but for her resonant actions. The way she maneuvered the monumental task of saving the library steeped him in profound respect for her. Louise surfaced from the library, venturing beyond, into the town, engaging with locals, and igniting a sense of shared responsibility towards the communal institution. Every whispered word, every heartfelt plea, every book recommendation she passed onto the townspeople painted a vivid picture of her resolve.

It was this spirited endeavor that stirred a chord within the heart of Charlie. He saw a reflection of himself in Louise, for he too, was soft-spoken, often catching himself lost in the pages rather than the bustling playground. Watching her leadership from the sidelines unknowingly planted a seed within his young heart, a seed of inspiration that began to sprout a resolve to bring about change in his own, quiet, unassuming way.

Charlie, a passionate animal lover, found his cause in the town's struggling pet shelter. He felt a deep kinship with the innocent creatures who found it their temporary haven. The shelter, although central to the wellbeing of countless abandoned pets in Picnic, was in dire need of assistance, with dwindling resources and soaring numbers of rescues. With the image of Louise's successful campaign at the forefront of his mind, Charlie decided to channel his empathy for these animals. He was determined to rally the town's support for the shelter, much like how Louise had done for the library.

Guided by the librarian's leadership journey, Charlie understood that his journey, like hers, would stem from love for his cause. He voiced his first, hesitant call-to-action to his school friends, employing Louise's practice of starting small - an echo of her delicate yet firm touch that instilled a sense of ownership and joy within the community. His earnestness, tranquillity, and passion shone through his words and actions, leaving an unforgettable impression on his friends, who began to see the silent potential in their usually shy and introverted companion.

Inspired, Charlie, like Louise, turned his attention to the wider community of Picnic. He repurposed his after-school hours, trading them for modest gatherings in homes or going door-to-door, creating an ambiance that reminded him of Louise's early meetings. Though he was merely a child, his enthusiasm and dedication shined brightly, deeply moving those he approached.

What started with sporadic homely meetings gained momentum as the people of Picnic came face-to-face with the boy's unwavering resolve for his cause. Familiar with the power of shared responsibility from their experience with the library, they began extending their support towards the pet shelter. Gradually, Charlie's passion project transmuted into a community-wide mission, fueled by the collective momentum that Louise had once ignited within them.

As the weeks turned into months, Charlie saw the resurrection of the pet shelter. Families opened their hearts and homes to abandoned animals, local businesses started sponsoring food and care, and the town increasingly participated in adoption drives. The once struggling pet shelter transformed into a thriving, nurturing haven, all due to Charlie's quiet yet resilient leadership.

Charlie's efforts became a testament to Louise's influence on the residents of Picnic, notably the younger generation. She had proven that leadership was not about grandeur but about unity, empathy, and relentless resolve. Charlie had not only understood but applied these principles, becoming a beacon of quiet leadership himself.

Louise's leadership had been contagious, infecting Charlie and, through him, the whole town. Looking around, he saw a picturesque town intertwined by shared responsibilities, collective love, and an unshakeable belief in the power of quiet leadership. Louise's influence had sparked a transformative journey in Charlie's life, enabling him to become a leader in his own right. In his quest to garner support for the shelter, he channeled her introverted leadership style, which was rooted in careful listening, humble negotiation, and an unfailing devotion to what they held dear.

The quiet librarian had once again become the cornerstone of a communal revolution, this time through Charlie, who steered his campaign on a course charted by Louise's example. He witnessed firsthand the infectious spirit of shared responsibility and quiet resilience she had first sown in Picnic's heart. Her leadership lived on, inspiring the townspeople to rally around a worthy cause - reinforcing the belief that leadership did not belong only to those who shouted the loudest, but also to those who spoke softly and with determination.

And so, as yet another beautiful day in the tranquil town of Picnic came to an end, Charlie stood in the thriving shelter, watching the rescued animals play merrily around him. He couldn't help but smile, realizing that he, a young, introverted boy, had successfully steered his town through a struggle, saving countless innocent lives, and transforming a dwindling pet shelter into a beloved communal institution. His heart filled with pride and gratitude for the quiet woman behind the library counter - Louise, the librarian whose quiet leadership had inspired him to harness the power within him to rally his beloved hometown behind a cause he cared deeply about. As he patted the head of a playful puppy, he knew that the story of his quiet leadership, borne out of the ashes of a beautiful legacy, would resonate through the ages, inspiring future generations of quiet but determined leaders to shine.

Analyzing The Quiet Influencer

In a world where assertiveness and demonstrative prowess often take center stage, the concept of leadership is predominantly associated with these extroverted qualities. Nonetheless, a deeper examination reveals that leadership can manifest in a myriad of ways, transcending the boundaries of extroversion and charisma. A case in point is the equally potent, yet often overlooked, form of leadership showcased by quiet, introverted individuals. These leaders navigate the complexities of life's challenges by relying on their innate traits of humility, persistence, and deep empathy. Louise, the introverted librarian from Picnic, serves as an example of this alternative perspective on leadership. Her inspiring story offers invaluable insights that shed light on the essence of introverted leadership and its far-reaching effects on communities and beyond.

Louise's journey illuminates the power of introverted leadership and its lasting impact on the fostering of strong, supportive communities. For instance, Louise's unwavering commitment to the preservation of the library breathes new life into this once-forgotten haven of knowledge. As a result, the community recognizes the significance of this institution, and the library becomes the bedrock of Picnic's evolving educational and intellectual landscape. This transformation highlights Louise's ability to influence others and achieve meaningful change through her quiet, unassuming approach.

Furthermore, Louise's story serves as a compelling narrative that disrupts traditional notions surrounding leadership. By presenting an introverted librarian as a pivotal figure who championed a worthy cause, the story opens the gates for a more nuanced and expansive view of leadership. This paradigm shift prompts the contemplation of the profound contributions of quiet and introspective individuals, valuing their impact as much as those of their extroverted counterparts.

Introverted leaders like Louise possess a distinctive set of qualities that contribute to their effectiveness in influencing and guiding others. Among these traits are patience, attention to detail, empathy, and a steely resolve that culminates in unparalleled determination. These characteristics enable introverted leaders to set a powerful example, inspiring their teams or communities organically rather than through forceful directives. Such an approach to leadership is inherently beneficial, offering several unique advantages.

Introverted leaders excel at forming deep, meaningful relationships, which, in turn, creates a strong foundation of trust and loyalty within teams or communities. Moreover, this style of leadership encourages autonomy, empowering individuals to assume responsibility and ownership of their own actions, decisions, and growth. The synergy between these aspects of introverted leadership renders it a highly effective conduit for lasting change. Despite being less conspicuous or openly expressive, these leaders create an environment of inclusivity by recognizing and appreciating the individuality of each team member or community participant.

In this relationship-driven context, trust burgeons, serving as the bedrock from which further growth and collaboration can be catapulted. When a leader earns the trust of their team, individuals are more likely to feel secure in expressing their ideas and taking calculated risks. This sense of psychological safety empowers them to engage openly and contribute constructively, accelerating collective and individual growth.

Furthermore, introverted leaders often encourage and nurture autonomy, emphasizing the importance of personal responsibility and ownership. Their leadership style is not one of micromanagement, but rather, they guide from the side, allowing individuals to explore their abilities and navigate challenges independently. This autonomy breeds resilience, flexibility, and creativity, propelling both personal and professional development.

Being an introverted leader means being a facilitator rather than a dictator, and this nurturing style creates an environment where individual growth and learning are celebrated. It instills a sense of accountability and fosters personal development, vitalizing both the individual and collective success of teams or communities.

The synergy between these attributes - fostering deep relationships, facilitating trust, promoting autonomy and growth - make introverted leadership an extraordinarily effective conduit for lasting and impactful change. Introverted leaders inspire transformation not through grand gestures, but through quiet persistence and a dedication to the individual and collective growth of their team or community. Indeed, the paradoxical power of an introverted leader lies in their silent affirmation of others' voices, insights, and potential.

Louise's personal odyssey movingly illustrates the potential of introverted leadership to spark profoundly transformative change. Her unwavering faith in the library's importance and her ability to galvanize the community around a shared vision offer irrefutable evidence of the efficacy of introverted leadership. Impressively, Louise's determination and quiet persistence trigger a profound transformation within the townspeople, shattering age-old stereotypes about leadership roles and capabilities.

In the wake of Louise's efforts, residents across Picnic are imbued with a renewed appreciation for the library's significance, as well as a deeper understanding of the impact that introverted leaders can have on their surroundings. Far from being a one-off phenomenon, Louise's legacy continues to inspire others within the community and beyond, cultivating an environment where quiet, humble determination is recognized as a driving force for change.

The stirring tale of Louise, the introverted librarian, invites its audience to redefine and broaden their understanding of leadership. By breaking free from the constraints of conventional wisdom, this narrative highlights the importance and relevance of introverted leadership in contemporary society. Introverted leaders like

Louise demonstrate that, through their humility, empathy, and unwavering commitment, profound change can be achieved.

Amidst a fast-paced, complex world, it is essential for readers to assimilate the insights gleaned from Louise's journey and recognize the quiet heroes in their own lives. By being mindful of diverse leadership styles and incorporating elements of introverted leadership in their own lives, individuals can contribute to a richer, more inclusive selection of change agents. Ultimately, embracing the full spectrum of leadership styles will empower society to forge innovative solutions that span demographics, build bridges, and facilitate progress. Whether the change is dramatic or imperceptible, every individual who dares to lead carries within them the catalyst for meaningful transformation. The key is to recognize this potential and use it to reshape the world — one quiet, determined step at a time.

THE UNOFFICIAL MENTOR

I n the heart of a sleepy town that barely roused itself in the sunlight lay Brilliant Brew—a quaint, cozy coffee shop, which was more like a secret treasure hidden away in the peaceful folds of the olden streets. The curious charm of the friendly brick-and-mortar store cheekily flirted with the nostalgia of its rustic roots, charmingly inviting those in search of respite and a bit of camaraderie, aside from the universal coffee rush.

Ah, the unmistakable lure of freshly ground coffee beans! How they wafted enticingly through the old, tall windows, painting the air with the rich aroma striking a familiar note of comfort while adding a dash of invigorating excitement about the tastes and conversations yet to unfold! Amidst the discreet noise of hushed exchanges, the slight clatter of cutlery and the quiet humming of espresso machines, there stood an unassuming beacon of nuanced inspiration—Donnie, the barista.

At first blush, one could mistake Donnie for any other diligent barista—taking orders, crafting beverages with practiced ease, all while casually swapping pleasantries with customers. But a closer look revealed the nimble ability of an individual who was adept not just in the art of perfect latte foam but also in the science of silent observation, attentive listening, sparking insightful conversations, and delivering timely wisdom. Donnie was not just about the beans and the brew; but an artful choreography of small actions, setting the stage for every interaction to morph subtly into an uplifting experience.

Donnie had mastered an uncommon art—the art of empathetic conversations that presented the luxury of feeling seen, heard, and understood. Visiting patrons found themselves sharing dreams, reluctance, setbacks, and victories over the counter as the empathetic barista poured coffee cups filled with warmth and words filled with wisdom. Donnie lent a thoughtful ear, shared comforting silence, cracked an encouraging joke, or offered a measured piece of advice; every act possessed a simple yet profound touch of human connection and kindness.

On a dreary Thursday afternoon, as melancholy trickled through the grey sky, Mark, an anxious undergraduate, tentatively approached the coffee counter. The captivating aroma of freshly-ground beans did little to lift his spirits, his eyes portrayed a troubled mind. Seeing him, Donnie immediately recognized the telltale signs of distress. However, he but echoed his usual cheerful, "What can I get you today?"

"Um, just a regular cup of joe, Donnie. Black." Mark responded, his voice barely a whisper.

While Donnie set to work, he invited Mark to join him at the counter. He began speaking casually, noting the downward curve of Mark's lips, the absent gaze. Through what might have seemed mundane banter about weather and books, Donnie gently stirred the conversation towards Mark's field of study, then his university life.

Mark, feeling heard for the first time in weeks, began to speak up. The burden of mismatched expectations tumbled forth—he confessed his dread about his chosen path in Engineering, his heart fluttered for Literature instead. His hands shook as he embraced his vulnerability in the safe space Donnie had created.

Donnie listened intently to every word, his face a mask of calm. When Mark finished speaking, he smiled gently, handing him his coffee, then a little sticky note he had been scribbling on. It read, "To leave behind the familiar is a test of courage. Embrace it."

Words of reassurance, empathy, and wisdom spun in a dance, pouring out of Donnie, illuminating Mark's pathway. The early words of a comforting barista on a gloomy afternoon brought a birth of courage in Mark's heart, pushing him towards the life he had dreamt.

A week later, Sarah, a recently promoted editor at a local publishing house, burst into the coffee shop. Anxiety poured off her in waves as she ordered her usual - almond milk cappuccino with an extra shot of espresso.

As he began to craft Sarah's beverage, Donnie sensed the tension crawling under her skin. His listening skills, honed over managing a coffee shop and countless conversations, kicked in by rote. More profound than the beans grinding or the music playing, he heard the unspoken stress making a home in Sarah's hurried words, clenched fists.

"Donnie, how do you manage all this?" the frustration echoed in her voice, gesturing at the coffee shop bustling with patrons.

A comforting smile curved Donnie's lips as he passed her the cup of cappuccino. He gestured for her to sit, then joined her after a few minutes. Over the soft jazz sighing in the background, Donnie shared his secret recipe - patience, passion for his work, embracing the messiness, and remembering to breathe. His humility and resilience wove a compelling testament to leadership, not thunderous but a silent symphony, which resonated with Sarah.

The conversation with Donnie was a pivotal moment for Sarah. His quiet wisdom, distilled over cups of coffee and a lifetime of observation, poured courage into her soul. His leadership - serene, solid as a rock yet fluid as a river, offered her the perspective she had overlooked.

Whilst gentle empathy helped Donnie connect with people at a unique, personal level, it was the careful sprinkling of wisdom and advice that truly distinguished their unconventional leadership style. From the morning's freshly brewed coffee and refreshing perspective to the twilight's calming decaf and comforting conversations, Donnie had different wisdom to offer at various parts of the day. Life lessons, motivational thoughts, pointed advice—an unconventional blend was served alongside each aromatic beverage.

And then it wasn't just about the coffee anymore. It was the customized sticky notes bearing motivational quotes, the gentle inquiry into someone's academic explorations or career progress, and the revealing of paths undreamt or unknown while Donnie navigated the labyrinth of coffee beans, milk froths, and human emotions with an apparent ease. His unique style did not align with the brimming bravado that was often the trademark of traditional leaders; instead, Donnie reflected a refreshing alternative —an unheralded hero subtly reshaping lives while going about their daily activities.

Just as the seasons subtly shift the scenery, transforming the landscape from a lush spectacle to a dramatic burst of colors and then to a peaceful portrait of pristine white, Donnie's presence began to transform the patrons' lives. The seemingly small interactions began rippling into noticeable changes: an undergraduate validating her course major, an office worker battling stress now sporting a calmer demeanor, a lonely old man rediscovering his passion for reading, and many more such instances. Donnie's quiet resilience to affect change persisted, his faith in people never faltering, his optimism never waning.

Such was the profound, resounding silence—or should we say the serenity—of Donnie's everyday heroism that it not only transformed the café into a safe haven for personal and interpersonal exploration but also began spilling over the town, subtle yet noticeable.

As the year passed, scores of people found themselves sharing their progress and setbacks with an air of bravery and honest acceptance. The burden of silent battles began lifting, making way for an exchange of understanding nods, heartening laughter, delighted high-fives, and sometimes, shared triumphant tears.

All through this transitional journey of little victories and occasional setbacks, the essence of quiet leadership began to unveil itself. It revealed a lesson simpler yet profound than any verbose proclamation of ambitions or declarations of change. It gently awakened a veneration for all the understated, thoughtful leaders who walked among us, not in the limelight but on the sidelines. These unassuming men and women shaped lives every day, leading from behind, prodding when someone needed a push, pulling when someone seemed to be rushing, serving guidance when someone lost their way, or simply sharing the quiet when someone yearned for their thoughts to be heard and understood.

Whether it was about handing someone their favorite coffee on a dismal day, extending a comforting pat guiding an individual to believe in themselves, or merely creating a shared space of acceptance where everyone felt safe and seen, Donnie became the face of the hidden, quiet leadership that flourished around us. And all he did was pour coffee and sprinkle conversations with kindness, compassion, and optimism.

In the fleeting moments that life offered, Donnie taught that leadership was not always a call to heroic acts or grand gestures; it was often about the subdued yet resounding whispers of empathy, guidance, and silent acts of caring.

In the story of a small town, a smaller coffee shop, and a simple barista, it was glaringly clear that leadership was not something that thundered always from the stage or roared from the apex. Many a time, it was a song sung by the audience, a story narrated from among the onlookers, or wisdom shared over a coffee counter. The real heroes were seldom in capes; more often, they wore aprons.

Silent Inspirations from The Unofficial Mentor

A regular at Brilliant Brew, Thomas was a mild-mannered individual with a profound passion for baking. He cherished the dream of opening his bakery but was held back by the whispering walls of his fears: the fear of failure, the fear of inadequacy, and the fear of stepping into the brutal world of entrepreneurship while leaving behind the relative comfort of his old but stable job.

As the seasons passed, the dream of 'The Aromatic Bakery' appeared like a distant star, gradually flickering, and fading as he faced the jarring realities of life, financial limitations, and the looming shadow of uncertainty. However, little did he anticipate that a beacon of change would emerge from the confines of his favorite coffee shop, Brilliant Brew.

Each interaction with Donnie, the barista and quiet leader of Brilliant Brew, proved to be an unforeseen therapy session for Thomas. As their conversations revolved around the familiar, comforting aromas of coffee beans and pastries, Thomas unconsciously began to pick up on Donnie's empathetic leadership style. He found himself pulling strength from Donnie's unwavering optimism, impressed by the calm, serene resilience displayed amidst the chaotic symphony of a coffee shop.

Donnie's subtle nuggets of wisdom, offered like essences distilled from a life rich in experiences, inspired Thomas. His fear began to ebb as he closely observed Donnie's leadership style. He saw the potential that resided in quiet tenacity, in the power of believing in one's skills, and the ability to embrace the intricacies of human emotions without losing sight of his dreams.

One winter evening, nursing a cup of warm coffee, Thomas looked around Brilliant Brew. He observed the camaraderie, the shared laughter, the comforting silence of people engrossed in their world, all woven together under Donnie's empathetic leadership. That sight acted as a catalyst, prompting a bold decision in Thomas— to venture into entrepreneurship and bring 'The Aromatic Bakery' from the realm of his dreams to reality.

With a newfound determination, he began formulating his business plan, ignited by his passion for baking and bolstered by the insights gained from Donnie's leadership style. Thomas took inspiration from Donnie's approach to connecting with people, understanding their unique tastes, preferences, and coupling that knowledge with his innate talent for baking.

In the heart of spring, Thomas finally opened the doors to his bakery— 'The Aromatic Bakery.' The venture's journey wasn't always smooth sailing; he faced multiple challenges, from supply chain disruptions to hiring and training his team. Yet, he found solace in remembering Donnie's calm meetings with adversity, using them as his guiding principles.

Encouraging open dialogue and fostering a culture of empathy within his bakery, Thomas began nurturing a team that resonated with his dream and passion. He worked long hours, honing his baking skills and keeping his team motivated. His assiduity reflected in the bakery's tantalizing pastry lineup, each item narrating a tale of meticulous craftsmanship.

The tactful combination of delicious pastry offerings, an inviting ambiance, and interactive customer service soon began to attract a crowd. 'The Aromatic Bakery' started garnering positive reviews and customer loyalty, laying the foundation for a thriving business. Thomas attributes his serendipitous entrepreneurial success to his decision that winter evening at Brilliant Brew and the indispensable lessons derived from Donnie's quiet leadership.

Through cumulative efforts, empathy-driven leadership, and undying perseverance, Thomas' dream blossomed from a mere vision into a commercially successful, people-centric bakery enterprise.

The narrative of Thomas' entrepreneurial journey brings forth a meaningful perspective on overcoming personal fears and venturing into the unknown with newfound enthusiasm. This transformative journey reflects the power of an empathetic leadership style, illustrating how it can inspire individuals not merely within its immediate sphere but far beyond. As Brilliant Brew stands as an enduring testament to Donnie's leadership, 'The Aromatic Bakery' became the embodiment of the far-reaching inspiration unfolded from the corners of a small coffee shop.

Whistling past the wind of life, the echoes of Donnie's quiet leadership found resonant strings in Thomas, inspiring him to surmount his fears, live his entrepreneurial dream, and make a significant impact in his community through a passion for baking. Donnie's quiet leadership style and the bustling strength behind 'The Aromatic Bakery' proved that leadership might lie in unexpected places, brewing over a cup of coffee, or blooming amid flour and baking aromas. It's a manifestation of courage, resilience, and a deep understanding of human connections, exhibited in the world that surrounds us.

Analyzing The Unofficial Mentor

In a certain sleepy town, tucked between everyday life and the extraordinary, stands the quaint coffee shop, Brilliant Brew. And at the helm of the coffee shop is an individual who, at first glance, may seem like an ordinary barista — Donnie. However, a closer look reveals compelling facets of leadership subtly displayed in Donnie's interactions with the patrons of Brilliant Brew. Donnie's story unfolds as a stark contrast to the conventional understanding of leadership. His role, far removed from the boardrooms and political arenas typically associated with leadership, offers a refreshing perspective; leadership can grace anybody's life, no matter where they stand, even if they are brewing and serving coffee for a living.

This analysis will delve into Donnie's quiet, empathetic style of leadership that imprints significant, lasting changes in individuals across a broad spectrum. It is aimed to highlight and explore the lesser-known aspects of leadership displayed in Donnie's actions and interactions — an effort to bring these ordinarily unobserved characteristics into the limelight, providing actionable lessons applicable to our lives.

If Donnie's unique style of leadership was distilled into a single concept, it would paint the clear picture of empathy. Going beyond the typical sympathetic reassurances often offered in passing, Donnie was deeply attuned to the patrons' emotions and experiences, actively engaging in resonating conversations that opened an avenue for genuine connection. Empathy was deployed not as merely listening passively to someone else's stories, but being truly present through each interaction, validating others' feelings, courageously sharing their raw emotions, and in doing so, kindling a profound interpersonal bond.

Another significant aspect of Donnie's leadership approach revolved around the timely dispensation of wisdom and thoughtful insights. This unique trait surpassed the general norms of advice giving and moved towards acting as a catalyst for introspection and self-realization. Rather than directly suggesting solutions, Donnie wielded his keen perceptiveness and a deep understanding of human behavior to offer profound insights, nudging individuals towards their 'aha' moments—moments when they came face-to-face with the truths of their dilemmas and were able to navigate their conundrums with renewed clarity.

Donnie's leadership approach was not exemplified in grand gestures or sweeping speeches. Instead, it resided in the gentle subtleties of routine interactions—conversations about dreams, challenges, joy, and fears held against the backdrop of swirling steam from freshly brewed coffee. The casual setting allowed patrons to let down their guards, openly exploring complex thoughts and emotions that they struggled to access otherwise. The humble coffee shop metamorphosed into an unexpected platform for introspection and self-improvement.

Perhaps the less noticeable thread that ran through the fabric of Donnie's leadership style was underscored resilience and optimism. Life, with its vast canvas, paints various scenarios wherein we're introduced to success and failure, joy and sadness, clarity, and confusion. Donnie showcased a definite determination and unruffled optimism to power through life's mixed hues and invariably believed in people's ability to grow and overcome adversities.

Under the caring guidance of Donnie's empathetic leadership, patrons took bold strides toward personal and professional growth. Donnie wasn't merely serving coffee or pastries but serving as a beacon lighthouse amid the stormy seas of doubts and insecurities of those contemplating life's choices. Whether it revolved around steering an undergraduate toward her career aspirations or helping a struggling office worker find his inner peace, Donnie's leadership touched lives across a vast spectrum, highlighting the universal relevance and the potentially transformative power of empathy-driven leadership.

Beyond the confines of Brilliant Brew's cozily lit ambiance, the influence of Donnie's empathetic leadership style permeated the town's residents, infiltrating everyday lives and conversations. The little coffee shop became a source of inspiration, a space facilitating open dialogue, camaraderie, shared laughter, and even the occasional collective tear — all sparked by Donnie's unique approach to leadership. His leadership rippled through the community, creating a lasting impact, and endorsing the idea that every individual has the power to be an agent of change, irrespective of their social or professional standing.

Through Donnie's story, one observes a refreshing perspective on the diverse manifestations of leadership. Donnie, as an unassuming barista, breathes life into Brilliant Brew, not just by serving warmth in a cup but by truly humanizing the role of a leader. This tale emphasizes that leadership isn't solely about charisma or authority. It's about sparking meaningful conversations over a simple cup of coffee, shaping the lives of those you interact with, and fostering a nurturing environment where growth and transformation flourish. It's about the quiet, empathetic, leaders like Donnie who, whilst standing at the edge of the grand stage of life, make significant, lasting ripples in the pool of humanity.

THE COMPASSIONATE CARETAKER

In the peaceful, rolling green fields of Iowa, a young girl named Patricia, or as everyone called her, 'Trish', emerged from a close-knit family where kindness was currency and love blossomed freely. Sweeping landscapes and tantalizing summer lemonade stands filled her days, while her compassionate grandmother's nurturing presence led her nights. Time spent with her beloved grandmother laid the foundation for a life of selflessness and boundless affection, culminating in her journey as a compassionate caretaker.

Trish's tender spirit was tested during her adolescence as she cared for her ailing grandmother. The hours spent consoling, nurturing, and connecting on a deeper level awoke a dormant passion within her. This significant period of her life revealed to her the true nature of caregiving, which went far beyond clinical needs and demanded an infusion of empathy, affection, and dignity in meeting the challenges faced by delicate souls. The flame ignited within her became the cornerstone of her destiny, setting her on a path toward empathetic leadership and transformative caregiving.

Upon joining the ranks of the nursing staff at Emerald Nursing Home, Trish seldom allowed herself a moment of respite between her countless obligations and responsibilities. It was her personal mission to fill the hearts and heal the souls of every resident, one smile, one story, one embrace at a time. Her angelic patience and tenderness resonated throughout the facility, elevating it from the confinement of a customary nursing home to the comforting safety of an undisputed sanctuary.

As a natural-born empath, Trish possessed a heightened ability to perceive and understand the turmoil endured by those suffering in silence. Like an expertly woven tapestry, she wove her own life seamlessly into the fabric of each resident's, color by color, thread by meticulous thread. With each interaction, she shone the bright light of her own spirit into the dark recesses of their hearts, a beacon of hope, love, and acceptance.

As the golden Iowa sunset filtered through the blinds of Emerald Nursing Home, Trish made her way towards room 208, home to her latest patient – Mr. Monte, fondly known as Arthur, the once-renowned violinist. Outside his room, she took a moment to gather herself, preparing for an encounter that could potentially be life-altering for both of them.

Being assigned to Arthur's case had been a surprise. His reputation not just as a musician, but as an older gentleman fraught with a formidable spirit and a heartbreaking inability to express it, had preceded him. Trish, however, was undeterred. As always, she led with her empathetic heart, eager to thread her patient's pain with her brand of compassionate and transformative caregiving.

Walking in, she was met with a scene that seemed right out of a beautifully somber symphony; Arthur sat by the window, gazing despondently at the violin resting silent but majestic on his lap, a testament to a past filled with applause, standing ovations, and soulful music. Sensing her presence, he turned his gaze towards her.

"You know, Trish," Arthur's voice was a quiet whisper, "the silence of this violin feels like a void in my soul. The music is still in me, but my hands... they fail me with every passing day."

Those words settled heavily within the room, a

melancholic note hanging in the air. Trish looked into Arthur's eyes, seeing a depth of despair that tugged at her compassionate heart. Taking a calming breath, she perched on the corner of his bed, tentatively reaching out to touch his arthritis-ridden hands, tracing the veins with a gentleness that seemed to momentarily ease his discomfort.

"Arthur," her voice rang clear and soothing, "our bodies might fail us, but our spirits - they're an orchestra hall replete with stories, experiences, and emotions. The silence of your violin doesn't negate the music within you."

His response was a meek nod—the first step towards understanding and acceptance. Here was Trish, etching the first strokes of their bond with empathy, leadership, and an unwavering belief in the power of compassion.

In the days that followed, Trish became Arthur's ray of hope. Her affectionate interactions didn't just end at clinical care or fulfilling duties. She soared beyond them, her empathetic approach breathing life back into his gloomy world. They would often chat about his concert days, his mischievous smiles and twinkling eyes when reminiscing. Trish became Arthur's safe haven, manifesting her compassionate and transformative leadership in the most heartfelt manner.

An inexplicable bond, sparked by the shared language of music, formed between Trish and Arthur. Beethoven's Minuet in G Major became the auditory bridge connecting a loving legacy to the rediscovery of purpose in the twilight of life. As Trish's calm and nurturing presence filled Arthur's heart with comfort, the harmonious melodies of his violin filled the nursing home with a vibrancy and warmth that permeated every corner.

Time, the relentless marcher of fate, brought with it a cruel reminder of mortality. Slowly yet steadily, Arthur's nimble fingers succumbed to the growing embrace of arthritis, forcing silence upon his once-powerful violin. A once-thriving spirit now faced the unbearable weight of despair and heartache. When darkness threatened to consume his world completely, it was Trish who intervened, and in doing so, showcased her unwavering commitment to compassionate leadership.

Realizing that Arthur's dwindling health and inability to play the violin were eating away at his very soul, Trish enlisted the aid of her fellow nurses and implemented a plan that would change the lives of all who called Emerald home. With a shared vision of unity, empathy, and love as the driving force, the residents and staff came together to organize a tribute evening to honor Arthur and his remarkable career as a violinist.

The Emerald community transformed into a garden of shared human experiences as each person contributed uniquely and wholeheartedly to the tribute. Bonds were forged, passion was ignited, and a renewed sense of purpose permeated the once-dormant atmosphere. Within this emotional embrace, a powerful, unspoken energy emerged, affirming the transformative power of collective compassion when guided by an empathetic leader.

As the tribute evening unfolded, the melodies created by young musicians reverberated within Arthur's frail frame and his soul. In that beautifully composed moment of time, tears streamed down his cheeks as memories, both cherished and mourned, swelled within his weakening heart. The eloquently executed performance of Minuet in G Major transported the entire gathering to an elevated plane of human connection, where laughter, heartache, and triumphs became one shared emotional truth. The evening's profound impact resonated deeply, leading to a newfound realization of the collective strength and healing power present within every kind and gentle touch, every comforting word, and every genuine embrace.

The weeks that followed served as a testament to the significance and beauty of this human experience, breathed to life under Trish's compassionate touch. Eyes that once harbored profound loneliness gleamed with a sense of belonging, while heavy hearts found solace in the genuine affection each resident received. The nurses themselves discovered within their profession a wellspring of limitless power, transcending their clinical duties to journey into the realm of healers born from empathy and connectedness.

Time, however, continued on its relentless march, weaving threads of loss and newfound appreciation into the living tapestry. Arthur's harmonious tunes and Trish's boundless compassion lived on in the hearts and souls of those touched by their loving presence. Though the melodies of Arthur's beloved violin and Trish's devoted caregiving eventually receded into the quiet of memory, their legacies lived on in each and every life transformed by their influence at Emerald Nursing Home.

In the annals of Emerald's history, the story of Trish and Arthur's unspoken bond remained a living testimony to the importance of compassionate leadership. They illuminated the path toward a life of unwavering dedication and kindness, creating ripples felt far and wide. Nurse Trish's journey revealed that true caregiving transcended the bounds of physical needs and spiritual sustenance, culminating in an opus of empathy, compassion, and purposeful human connection—an extraordinary and transformative force that resonated through the very essence of life itself.

Compassion is Contagious

In the warm embrace of Emerald Nursing Home, Pamela, fondly known as Pam, felt a thrilling sense of rebirth. As the Activities Director, she had the vital responsibility of engaging the residents in meaningful activities that enriched and enlivened their lives.

Her diligent nature and cheerful disposition had made her a beloved presence among staff and residents alike. Her enthusiasm was contagious, and she had unlocked a new way of living through her interactions with the home's residents. However, seeing Trish in action made her reevaluate her role at Emerald, realizing that her job demanded much more than crafting event calendars, setting up festive decorations, and reciting cheerful announcements. Pam became acutely aware of the boundless potential of her position to truly impact lives, embracing the possibility of empowering change within the very essence of Emerald.

As Pam melded into the molds of life encompassing Emerald, she sought to emulate Trish's awe-inspiring compassion. Trish's ceaseless kindness had a profound impact on Pam, fueling an urgent yearning to transform her professional life and, in turn, the lives of the residents within her care. Pam observed as Trish went beyond the boundaries of obligation by offering unwavering emotional support to the delicate and weary souls seeking solace at Emerald. Guided by Trish's compassionate leadership, she began to nurture a deeper understanding of the art of caregiving.

Pam first flexed her newfound capacity for compassion during her interactions with Mrs. Margaret Roundtree, a fiercely independent resident whose vivacity for life had begun to whither under the weight of encroaching dementia. As the connections to her past slowly started slipping away, she was left with frail threads of memories woven into an intricate emotional quilt she desperately clung to for solace. With debilitating fear threatening to consume her, it was Pam who intervened, offering reassurances and patient understanding.

Giving of herself fully, Pam gifted Mrs. Roundtree with renewed purpose and joy by initiating activities that rekindled her love for painting and gardening. The creative endeavors, once inseparable from her identity, became her life's center once more. Under Pam's patient guidance, an artistic and tenacious soul found solace in the nurturing touch of color-laden brushes and the comforting embrace of warm, damp earth.

As her leadership evolved, Pam's new perspective extended beyond the walls of Emerald, weaving its way into the fabric of her personal life. Her genuine capacity for empathy found its way into every conversation, every embrace, and every ounce of affection given to those she loved. In transforming her approach to caregiving, Pam discovered that a life lived with compassion was a life of limitless potential for growth and genuine connections.

Upon witnessing the profound impact of Arthur's tribute night, conceived and executed with Trish's empathetic dedication, Pam suddenly found herself at a crossroads. The overwhelming unity and rejuvenation resonating throughout the nursing home stirred something deep within her – a rekindled flame, similar in essence to the one sparked within the heart of Trish herself. Pam realized that, as Activities Director, she wielded the potential to not only create events but to craft powerful, transformative experiences that breathed life, love, and newfound purpose into both the nursing home's residents and staff.

Under the nurturing guidance of Trish's unwavering compassion, Pam's role as Activities Director underwent a metamorphosis. No longer was she merely a facilitator of events, but a beacon of hope that illuminated the path toward a life of genuine connection, understanding, and mutual growth.

In one of Pam's initiatives, she invited the resident families to a "Family Talent Showcase," where residents and their loved ones gathered to demonstrate their unique gifts and passions on stage. Fueled by her desire to further the bonds between residents and their families, Pam's creation was a loving nod toward Trish's gentle influence.

Her compassionate leadership style radiated a transformative energy that spread to the Emerald staff, who began to incorporate empathy and understanding into their daily interactions. Unbeknownst to her, Pam had touched the lives of countless individuals, not only within Emerald's tranquil walls but within the larger community as well.

Pam soon felt the rewarding impact of her newfound compassionate leadership in her home life. Within the warmth of her family, where contentment, understanding, and love blossomed freely, every single interaction seemed to be woven together with harmony. Pam's young son blossomed into a kind, empathetic young man, the gentle touch of her compassionate leadership guiding him as he navigated the joys and struggles of youth.

He brought Pam's teachings to his school, where his empathy and support touched the lives of his friends and classmates, each bathed in the warm light of an upbringing rooted in love. Pam's teenage daughter, once teeming with silent rebellion, found solace in the newfound connection with her mother, resulting in a nurturing emotional bond that transcended the barriers of adolescent insecurity.

In her work at Emerald, Pam continued to craft transformative experiences for the home's residents, the hum of a renewed, infectious cheer that filled the hearts of everyone involved. Through her compassionate leadership, events that transcended the mundane became life-changing experiences that ignited the flames of hope, love, and purpose within countless lives.

The artistic, expansive nature of her role within Emerald continued to provide Pam with a richness and depth of connection she could have only dreamt of before. Through her devotion to compassion, understanding, and genuine human connection, she forged an expansive web of relationships that spanned generations, lifting the hearts and spirits of both the young and the old.

As Pam's compassionate leadership took flight, so too did the powerful bonds and connections she left behind. Deep-rooted empathy and understanding bloomed within the hearts of both staff and family members, creating an interwoven community bound together with love, compassion, and hope—a new, golden age of genuine connection at Emerald. Pam's transformation illuminated the power and far-reaching impact of a life guided by love, kindness, and grace.

The journey of Pamela as the Activities Director of Emerald Nursing Home showcased the transformative power of empathy and compassionate leadership, a living testament to the legacy of Patricia. As the experiences and connections Pam had forged began to reverberate within the community, it was evident that Trish's gentle touch had left an indelible print. And after every heartfelt embrace, every tearful laugh, and every whisper of hope, Pam's life stood as powerful evidence that true caregiving transcended roles, embracing the beauty of a life guided by compassion and understanding—a legacy lived on through the hearts of all it touched.

Analyzing the Compassionate Caretaker

At the heart of the transformative stories of Patricia and Pamela is a unique breed of leadership: compassionate leadership. Theirs is not a conventional leadership style bound by the scope of work, position, or power dynamics. Rather, their unique style transcends these boundaries, weaving together elements of empathy, understanding, and human connection. Their leadership is marked by a profound person-centered approach that places the well-being of those under their care front and center.

Trish's role as an experienced and empathetic nurse exemplified compassionate leadership. She exceeded the defined boundaries of her duty to build personal, meaningful connections with her patients. Trish's ability to perceive the unspoken needs of those she cared for, such as their emotional well-being, exemplified a deep-rooted empathy that goes unnoticed among many others. By recognizing these hidden needs and acting to address them, she positively changed the lives of countless individuals under her care.

Observing this unique form of leadership firsthand, Pam, the dedicated Activities Director at Emerald Nursing Home, began to mold her role in the same vein. Inspired by Trish's approach, Pam infused her work with an unparalleled level of empathy and understanding. Instead of viewing her job as mere routine, she approached her activities like an artist envisions a masterpiece. Each event, each activity, was a unique opportunity to create memories that transcended the mundane and touched the lives of Emerald's residents at a profoundly human level, instilling a deep sense of purpose.

The importance of compassionate leadership cannot be overstated due to its capability to transform an organization's culture. It helps create an environment which champions humanity's most cherished qualities: empathy and understanding. This form of leadership can not only increase employee satisfaction, encourage mutual understanding, and improve overall organizational effectiveness, but it also fosters an atmosphere that promotes personal growth, productivity, and nurturing relationships. It creates an organizational culture that values collaboration and understanding, reinforcing the human element in professional endeavors.

In a healthcare setting like Emerald Nursing Home, compassionate leadership stands out as particularly significant. Healthcare professionals regularly interact with individuals who find themselves in vulnerable states - they may be aging, battling illness, or coping with personal challenges. In such an atmosphere, compassionate leadership becomes pivotal to the well-being of all involved. In a world often dictated by clinical necessities, Trish and Pam painted an alternate picture, one where compassionate leadership shines.

Compassionate leadership doesn't limit itself to professional confines; it cascades into personal lives as well, making it a phenomenally effective form of leadership. Much like a steady cascading waterfall nourishes all that lies in its path, a compassionate leader nurtures their environment with a formidable blend of trust, respect, and loyalty. Creating a positive effect where everyone feels valued, seen, and appreciated, a compassionate leader fosters an atmosphere conducive to both personal and professional growth.

With Trish and Pam at the helm, Emerald Nursing Home thrived, exhibiting improved levels of engagement and positivity amongst residents and caregivers. Both Trish's intuitive understanding of her patients' needs and Pam's empathetic approach towards creating engaging experiences painted a vivid portrait of the effectiveness of compassionate leadership.

Being compassionate can enhance emotional wellbeing and reduce distress. Upon observing Trish's compassion, patients like Arthur found acceptance and solace, and were able to appreciate life despite their physical limitations. Pam's initiatives breathed new life into the routine of many residents at Emerald, fostering a sense of belonging and happiness. This greatly improved their emotional health and overall sense of satisfaction.

Compassionate leadership builds trust within a community. Leaders like Trish and Pam cultivated trust through their consistent demonstration of understanding, empathy, and genuine care for the residents. Their compassionate leadership fostered a thriving, empathetic community and improved the quality of life for all residents of Emerald. Crucially, compassionate leadership also influences personal growth. With Trish as her inspiration, Pam experienced a personal transformation that touched her professional and personal life, including her evolving relationship with her children. This deep-seated connection between leadership style and personal growth underpins the potency of compassionate leadership.

The lives of Trish and Pam bear testimony to the transformative power of compassionate leadership. It is a type of leadership that permeates every facet of life, sparking genuine connections, creating enduring change, and reshaping the essence of communities. This leadership style channels the core strength of human empathy and goodwill for the betterment of all.

Their stories are striking examples of the effectiveness of compassionate leadership. They present a compelling argument for why compassionate leadership needs to be more widely embraced. A human-centered approach to leadership that fosters harmonious, empathetic work environments, compassionate leadership cultivates an intimate, tightly knit community that only emerges from the profound resonance of genuine human connections.

THE NIGHT SHIFT SAGE

The moon was a crescent in the subtle velvet painting that was the night sky. Stars politely flickered, vying for attention, but their glamour was drowned in the glow of terrestrial existence — the artificial world that is factory life. At the heart of this industrial sprawl vibrated a colossus of metal and smoke: the Cane Factory. The very manifestation of contemporary civilization's progress — and its relentless demands.

Amid these titanic fortresses of industry toiled a man: a night shift worker named James. Aged in the late forties, he had become a familiar figure in the labyrinthine landscape of conveyor belts and dreams. In him, the clamor of the factory found a tempering harmony, a rhythm resounding with the pulse of human aspiration. He was a night laborer, a weaver of dreams in the empire of necessity.

His home beyond the factory was a humble abode radiating the warmth of his heart, lovingly shared with his wife and two kids. Having lost his father quite early, James had always been thrust with responsibilities that charted the course of his natural growth to be kind, nurturing, empathetic, and, most importantly, accountable. It was these individual threads delicately woven together along the fabric of his persona that presented an intriguing idea of leadership: a leadership that had the tenacity to command authority, yet consciously chose to dwell beneath the obvious.

As the slumbering day gave way to the peaceful quietude of the collegial night, James, along with numerous other laborers, breathed life into the dormant factory. Here, amidst the hum of machines and half-stifled dreams, James discovered the intent of his leadership and the echoes of his purpose.

Every night, under the cold luminescence of fluorescent lighting, James found himself immersed in the ceaseless rhythm of machinery and the silent ballet of night shift operations. Tireless arms swayed to the rhythm, hoisting loads, directing assemblies, and leading quiet rebellions against the weary hours of body-breaking labor.

While most eyes were on the clock, awaiting

respite, James' eyes danced around the tired, soulful gazes of his comrades. He saw weary bodies pushing against time, spirits swaddled in fatigue, and an undercurrent of resignation to this relentless grind. This was the canvas where he chose to cast the seeds of change, one subtle, transformative deed at a time.

Fired with an intent stoked by empathy, James set about crafting his revolution in the quietly magnificent theater of the night shift. He began with observation, feeling the pulse of the assembly line, and understanding the unspoken ethos that held this orchestration of labor and longing together. He paid attention to his colleagues, listening to their stories, their concerns, and their dreams that fluttered like moths under the severe spotlight of reality.

James realized the night shift wasn't just a group of workers, but a 'communal entity' with shared challenges, aspirations, and triumphs. Recognizing this, he took on responsibilities beyond his own, sharing the load of his colleagues whenever possible. He held his hand out to struggling colleagues, not standing above but shoulder-to-shoulder, equal in burden and in triumph.

Every night, he quietly pushed against the inertia of despair, cheering his fellow workers forward, always offering his kindness and support.

His tireless cheerfulness, the warmth of his broad smile, the calming tone of his voice often acted as the much-needed balm to soothe the chafed spirits and tired hearts of his fellow factory workers.

It was never about wielding command, issuing orders, or claiming credit for James. He preferred to steer his colleagues toward positive changes indirectly, subtly buffering their paths from obstacles rather than loudly proclaiming his prowess. He set about making his intentions visible through actions rather than words, his deeds leaving a gentle yet profound impact.

He facilitated his colleagues to take ownership of their workspace, promoting a sense of belonging, pride, and shared accountability. Instead of pushing his thoughts, he respectfully acknowledged their ideas, fostering a sense of validation, and subtly steering further improvements.

His ethos of shared responsibility culminated in a compelling narrative of increased job satisfaction, co-worker bonding, and even a marked decrease in the employee turnover rate. Workers no longer felt like expendable parts of an immense machine but valuable threads in a rich, shared tapestry. It was a shift not just in their circumstance but in their perspective, and it all came about due to James's unassuming yet potent leadership.

As the symphony of machinery filled the air, beneath the stark white fluorescence of the night factory, George, a junior ranking coworker, was struggling. Hunched over conveyor belt #6, the creases on George's forehead deepened, his palms sweaty with unusual pressure. An unstacked pallet of materials marked the glaring interruption in the seamless rhythm of the tightly choreographed production line.

Seeing this unusual ruffle, James, otherwise immersed in his nightly duties, crossed over to George's station. His approach was devoid of any ostentatious authority. Instead, it communicated a quiet intent to support, much like an elder brother stepping up to help his struggling sibling.

He gently placed a comforting hand on George's shoulder, offering a reassuring smile - his warmth, like a dose of reassurance. "Everyone hits a stumbling block once in a while, George," he said, deftly stacking the materials, his skilled hands moving seamlessly with the rhythm of the conveyor belt. "What matters is, we face the challenge together."

As James guided George, it wasn't a dictation but an exchange of experiences. He fueled George's agency, reminding him that everyone here held an equal stake, and implying that it was not George's individual lapse, but a temporary lull in the entire team's rhythm. This spirit of shared responsibility, an undercurrent in James's leadership, inspired George to realign himself with the existing communal entity.

His consistent respect for every individual and the subtle shifts he instigated fostered a culture of shared burden and triumph. It was this shift in perspective that thawed George's initial embarrassment. The shy demeanor shed itself, replaced by an aspiration to share this responsibility heralded by James and his humble leadership.

Despite a busy shift, James gave George his time, demonstrating his empathetic nature. His accessibility and willingness to extend a helping hand, regardless of hierarchy, added to his leadership's unique definition. He subconsciously encouraged George to perceive his role beyond a routine 'job' and more as a cherished 'responsibility'.

As the months rolled on and seasons left behind their echoes, change whispered through the night shift. It was never an abrupt transformation—rather, a slow, beautiful unfolding much like dawn replacing night. Morale bloomed among the workers, the air became less tense, laughter and camaraderie displaced the discomfort of long monotonous hours. The factory no longer represented just an integral pillar of vast industrial machinery—it had transformed into a cradle fostering human connection and nurturing a sense of purpose.

While the machinery echoed the symphony of industry, James was silently orchestrating a symphony of humanity, one note at a time. He was finely tuning the sublime music of empathy, kindness, and shared responsibility that began filling the once monotonous nights with a newfound positivity. His life was the testimony of an often-overlooked premise—that leadership could flower in the most unexpected soils. It required no grand stages to prove its worth yet subtly impacted the very fabric of shared experiences.

Admittedly, James's poetic saga of transforming an industrial night shift wouldn't show up in conspicuous chronicles of leadership. But in the theme of everyday heroism set on the nocturnal stage of the factory, etched in every pair of twinkling, hopeful eyes, and imprinted on every heart that once beat with despair but now pulsed with positivity, his legacy thrived.

Night shift duties were grueling, but even within this demanding environment, the influence of sincere kindness, empathy, and shared purpose could significantly transform the collective and individual realities of workers. Leadership resided not necessarily within the glory of titles but often in the subtleties of human connection and the unassuming profundity of everyday actions.

The tale of James echoes a profound understanding of leadership—the power to facilitate positive change, the strength to inspire, and, most crucially, the courage to act out of compassion for the collective good. Subtle yet deeply transformative, it is in powerful narratives like James's that the true essence of leadership unveils itself—an unassuming ripple capable of instigating a wave of lasting impact.

Through James's journey, the leadership discourse receives a nuanced layer. It demonstrated the powerful potential of anyone, anywhere, irrespective of their title, role, or circumstances, to make a difference. Far beyond the visibly grand acts, it is often through the subtlety of our shared experiences, the authenticity of our intentions, and the consistency of dedication that we unintentionally yet powerfully manifest our leadership.

Indeed, leadership is a journey, unfolding and developing in profound ways, often from the most unexpected of places. And in the heart of an industrial nocturnal orchestra, amidst the synergistic symphony of human spirits, James, the Night Shift Sage, quietly scribed his testament of leadership—a testament that was less about managing resources and more about nurturing hearts, less about dictating terms and more about fostering dreams, and where success wasn't measured in production margins but in the luminous smiles that began breaking the monotony of the night shift. The factory was no longer just a site of labor but a canvas of transformative leadership, uplifting moments, and timeless impact.

In the language of whispers, actions, and kindness, the poetry of leadership was crafted with eloquence, wrapped in the veil of subtlety and dedication by none other than James. His narrative is a timeless reminder to all that leadership thrives not only in the boardrooms, not just in the acclaimed corridors of power and privilege, but often in the unnoticed corners of our everyday existence. It reverberates within our shared experiences, echoes within every act of compassion, and speaks through the silent language of empathy and understanding.

James, the factory worker, was a testament to the kaleidoscope of leadership, reflecting that sometimes, the most potent leadership insights and skills could indeed be sourced from where you least expect it. His sphere of influence, his stage may have been limited to the sprawling factory under the calmness of the night. Still, his legacy, radiating with profound leadership traits, proved to be remarkably universal and destined to transcend the limited notions of time and space. This indeed was the everyday leadership anthem of the Night Shift Sage, an anthem that echoed through the labyrinthine expanse of factory halls and reverberates in the hearts that he touched, leaving behind a legacy brilliantly cloaked in the subtleties of kindness, empathy, and shared responsibility.

Sage Wisdom

Within the vibrant ensemble of the factory's bustling narrative, two striking figures emerged. James, a night shift laborer, was a beacon of unexpected leadership. He wasn't deemed a leader by any official countenance, but his influence amidst his fellow night-shift workers was palpable. Without him, there was a notable lack of rhythm in the mechanical choreography of the night, and the factory floor didn't hum in quite the same synchronicity.

Contrasting the quiet personality of James was the radiant personality of Julie, the tireless HR representative of the factory. Despite being confined to daytime operations, Julie's influence was profound, serving as a guardian of the workforce. She was the last resort for resolving disputes, a helping hand in times of need, a listening ear during grievances, and a representative of the organization's human aspect.

Caught in the day-shift routine, Julie began to

perceive a shift in the work floor's ambience. What was once a discordant symphony of grumbling drones and tired sighs transformed into harmonious whispers of comradeship, collaborative achievements, and soaring job satisfaction. External to the factory floor, the change was subtle, yet perceptible, piquing her interest.

Being a seasoned HR professional, Julie knew better than to ignore the undercurrents running through her workforce. Dedicating one evening to delve into the mystery of the night-shift transformation, she stepped onto the nocturnal theatre of the factory floor. The dance of the night shift, orchestrated by James, was a revelation. It wasn't the stark reality of a factory's gritty underbelly, but a harmonious portrait of collective endeavor orchestrated by unspoken leadership.

James led with a humble confidence that drew coworkers closer, fostering a sense of camaraderie. He worked alongside them, shared their dilemmas, and resolved hurdles impartially. An observant listener, James spoke less but conveyed more. His actions echoed respect, empathy, support, and shared accountability; he was guiding, not commanding — solving, not ordering.

Julie watched this symphony with renewed fascination. Moved by the profound subtlety of

James' leadership, Julie saw an opportunity. It was a wake-up call for her to transform her role, not just as an HR representative, but as an empathetic collaborator with her workforce.

In the subsequent weeks, Julie undertook the challenge of redefining her HR role in the daylight echo of the factory. From meetings to floor rounds, she embodied the empathetic leadership observed in James. She engaged with each worker as equals, fostering honest and heartfelt conversations. The HR department, under her guidance, reveled in shared decision-making, harnessed employee engagement, and recognized proactive contributions—echoing the themes of mutual respect, shared growth, and empathy.

Amid the daylight hours, she choreographed a parallel dance to the nocturnal symphony, harmonizing the factory's pulse. The HR department dramatically improved, thus lowering churn rates and amplifying job satisfaction, all weaving the narrative of a more human-centric factory floor.

However, the transformation wasn't limited to Julie's personal enlightenment and her immediate HR department. Its ripples extended far beyond.

During an open mic session at one of the factory's town hall meetings, Julie decided to share her nocturnal encounter. She spoke eloquently about the subtle, transformative leadership that thrived in the night-shift realm under James' unassuming guidance. She narrated her own journey of transformation, detailing her shift from hierarchical supervision to empathetic collaboration.

The effect on the audience was profound. Factory workers began to think less of Julie as a distant administrative figure and more as an ally—a compassionate link between their ranks and the authoritative echelons. Managers, too, were moved by Julie's powerful narrative, finding merit in her model of leadership that transcended the conventional boundaries of authority and management. The shared stories encouraged them to revisit their leadership style, instigating a silent revolution within the entire organization.

The ensuing weeks saw an appreciable paradigm shift within the management. Guided by Julie's example, managers started reaching out more to their subordinates, smoothing the layers of hierarchy and fostering an environment of shared responsibility. Supervisors began walking the factory floors, engaging with their teams beyond the confines of their cubicles. More importantly, they started listening, really listening, to their subordinates, honoring their insights, and acknowledging their contributions.

Simultaneously, as James' subtlety of leadership became an everyday epitome, the nocturnal and the daytime realms of the factory began reflecting similar harmonies. They created an osmosis of compassion, respect, cooperation, and shared responsibility, making the factory a living testament of human-led leadership. It was a factory that did not just manufacture products but also cultivated a culture of collective welfare and empathetic leadership.

In the grand scheme of leadership, James and Julie personified two striking threads. As James wove his nocturnal narrative with empathy and kindness, Julie echoed the same during the daylight hours. Their influence, although subtle, was striking, reshaping the factory's larger narrative. Amidst this transformation, a potent leadership philosophy was born, reflective of true empathy, mutual respect, and shared ownership. It gently whispered that leadership wasn't exclusive to titles or hierarchy but inherent in every individual's ability to connect, care, and collaborate with others on a shared journey, under the canopy of shared dreams and ambitions.

Analyzing the Night Shift Sage

Amidst this panorama, two characters emerge with an intriguing narrative - James, an unassuming night-shift worker, and Julie, a formidable HR representative. Their story lays bare a leadership paradigm markedly different from traditional norms; this paradigm, characterized by empathy, collaboration, and mutual respect, tells us a significant tale about effective leadership. To illuminate the intricacies of such leadership styles, it is essential to delve into their characters and draw upon the events that unfold.

James presides over the factory's nocturnal life but is no official leader. His influence emanates subtly and distinctly through his style of leadership born out of an intuitive understanding of his co-workers and their surroundings. His empathic resonance with the workers shines throughout the shifts he oversees, meticulously marked by an environment of collaboration and understanding, a testament to his leadership acumen.

At the core of his leadership style is an all-encompassing empathy - he doesn't oversee the workers but actively involves himself in their experiences, aspirations, and grievances. He doesn't command; he guides, fostering an environment where workers feel understood and validated. His leadership resonates with the concept of "servant leadership," propounded by Robert K. Greenleaf in 1970.

Servant leaders, like James, prioritize their team members' growth, needs, rights, and voice. They actively involve their teams in decision-making, creating an empowering atmosphere conducive to personal and professional growth. By prioritizing empathy and understated leadership, servant leaders like James foster a motivating and empowering ethos, stimulating productivity and collaboration.

In the daylit sphere of the factory, Julie's universe debuts. Julie, touched by James' unique leadership style, embodies another vibrant manifestation of leadership - transformational leadership. Driven by James's example, Julie strategically lowers the walls of formal interaction and hierarchy to create an environment characterized by warmth, empathy, and inclusivity.

Julie's transformation from her traditional HR role to a transformational leader mirrors the principles of the 'Four I's Concept of Transformational Leadership' as popularized by Bernard M. Bass. These principles include Intellectual Stimulation, Individualized Consideration, Inspirational Motivation, and Idealized Influence.

Understanding the importance of these leadership styles is vital in comprehending their broad applicability across different types of leaders. The underlying principle of both James and Julie's leadership styles is the emphasis on people; they prioritize individuals over processes, nurturing an environment of trust, understanding, and collaboration.

For example, a leader in the context of a tightly knit technical team can utilize a servant leadership approach to understand the team's capabilities and aspirations, enabling them to optimize task allocation based on skill sets and inherent interests. Similarly, a transformational leadership approach, like that of Julie, can inspire and stimulate team members, creating positive working relationships and leveraging individuals' potentials.

The effectiveness of James and Julie's leadership styles is marked not just by their transformative influence on individual workers, but through their invigoration of the very ethos of the factory's workforce. Under James's 'Servant Leadership' approach, the night-shift operations are rejuvenated. Shared responsibility, mutual respect, trust, and empathy replace an ambiance of dissatisfaction, low morale, and tension.

In parallel, Julie's transformational leadership yields profound impacts across the factory's daylight operations. Her approach encapsulates empathic and transformational leadership principles, forming stronger connections with her workforce. In effect, the HR department transitions, under her guidance, from an administrative command center to a warm, welcoming hub fostering human connectivity, collaboration, and inclusivity.

The effectiveness of their leadership approaches is also substantiated by measurable key performance indicators such as improved job satisfaction, reduced staff turn-over, elevated workforce productivity, and an overall positive shift in the workforce culture.

The true measure of their leadership style's effectiveness is evident in the qualitative changes —the shift towards a more empathetic, respectful, and inclusive work culture. Such an environment, characterized by shared responsibility and ownership, equality, justice, and respect, is the crowning achievement and legacy of their empathetic leadership style.

The success of James and Julie's leadership styles goes beyond just their immediate sphere of influence. Their leadership philosophy resonates throughout the organization, setting the tone for a larger structural and cultural transformation. They are potent examples of how empathetic and transformational leadership can bring about significant positive changes even on a larger scale. Their narrative serves as an embodiment of servant and transformational leadership styles —demonstrating their principles and applicability in practical and real-world scenarios.

A key takeaway from their story revolves

around the idea that the ability to lead compassionately and effectively depends not on authority ordinated by hierarchy but rather on the individual's values and behavior. Their narrative is a compelling case of empathetic leadership creating transformative changes within the working environment—changes that not only boost productivity but also foster unity, trust, and respect among all players.

These overlooked corners of everyday work environments are where the most influential leaders can often be found. Sculpted and inspired by their surroundings, life experiences, and the wisdom to understand and act accordingly, they demonstrate that leadership, adaptability, and empathy can truly shape an organization.

The blend of James and Julie's leadership styles sketches a progressive canvas, a union of the nocturnal symphony and daylit echoes- a testament to leadership's ubiquitous characteristics. Their story underlines that leadership is a continuously evolving journey of self-discovery and transformation, which, when inspired and shared, illuminates the paths toward profound impacts in the most unexpected directions.

THE GENTLE GIANT

In the sprawling concrete jungle of New York City, where lofty skyscrapers stand like proud sentinels piercing the blue heavens, a humble worker named Eugene was hard at work in his trade. His towering form, though seemingly imposing at first glance, was veiled by his gentle, calm demeanor. Eugene's hard hat was adorned with simple words, little mementos acting as daily reminders of his core principles—phrases like 'Safety First' and 'Teamwork Makes the Dream Work'. They were concise but meaningful, forming the backbone of his deeply held personal values.

Eugene was no high-ranking official or renowned expert; he was an ordinary construction worker, putting on his well-worn boots each day to enter the world of steel, sand, and concrete. Instead of wielding a pen or tapping on a keyboard, Eugene's tools were simple, forged from iron and alloys. But in this potentially harsh and demanding environment, his style of leadership was as gentle as a soft summer breeze, uniting the individual workers like strings on a safety net—all working in harmony to ensure their collective protection.

Without any official authority or indication of rank, Eugene did not wield his power with an iron fist or issue threatening ultimatums. Instead, his leadership emanated from a deep well of empathy, patience, and understanding. His commitment to creating a safe workspace was not primarily driven by an instinct for self-preservation or an excessively cautious nature. It sprang from a profound sense of responsibility towards the safety and well-being of his fellow coworkers— a palpable altruism that silently transformed him into a guardian angel of sorts, one whose presence remained largely unnoticed but was of immense value, nonetheless.

Even when dawn had yet to break, as the first tendrils of sunlight just began to caress the skeletal steel framework of the impending architectural marvels in progress, Eugene had already plunged headlong into his meticulously planned safety checks. Each day began not with the sounds of pounding hammers or groaning machinery but with his studious, methodical inspection of equipment, gears, and harnesses. Step by step, he reinforced the importance of adherence to safety guidelines and protocols, ensuring that no detail was left to chance.

In the cacophonous symphony of construction, where hollering machines and clanging metal intertwine, Eugene navigated the labyrinth of potential hazards, always thinking one step ahead to protect his team. Knowing full well that his workspace was a minefield of possible disasters, he carried out his daily duties with unyielding resolve. He wasn't solely focused on his own well-being; instead, he dedicated himself to safeguarding the lives and livelihoods of the entire crew, shielding them from the gargantuan demands that each task placed on their shoulders.

Eugene's actions, though subtle and understated, did not go unnoticed. They reverberated throughout the ranks of his team, igniting a transformation that touched every single coworker. One such shift was the metamorphosis of Harry, a seasoned worker with years of experience under his belt. Initially, the safety measures that Eugene religiously adhered to seemed like little more than an unnecessary hassle to Harry, who, in his confidence and expertise, was comfortable cutting corners. But a near-fateful encounter with faulty scaffolding served as a visceral reminder of the importance of safety, upending Harry's cavalier attitude in an instant.

In a heartbeat, the precarious scaffolding that

Harry leaned against gave way, triggering a domino effect of collapsing steel and metal that surged towards the workers below. Amidst the chaos, Eugene sprang into action, his rapid response and intervention averting a major catastrophe. Not only did he ensure the safety of his crew, but he also took preventative measures to minimize the risk of future accidents.

That heart-stopping moment seared itself into Harry's memory, forever altering his perception of workplace safety. In witnessing Eugene's level-headed response and unwavering commitment to the well-being of his crew, Harry's prior dismissiveness gave way to a newfound respect for the principles championed by Eugene.

The scaffolding incident proved to be a watershed moment for the entire site. Eugene's unending advocacy for safety and well-being resonated with the team, sparking a collective shift in focus. Workers who had once put productivity above all else now recognized the critical importance of balancing their personal responsibilities with the need for a secure and healthy work environment. And as this understanding took root, it unified the disparate individuals once pitted against one another into a cohesive unit, harmoniously working together to achieve their shared goals.

But Eugene's influence didn't stop there. It

permeated through the layers of the organization, eventually catching the attention of the managerial forces in their remote offices. John Basker, a site supervisor known for his no-nonsense approach, was the first to acknowledge the subtle revolution that Eugene had sparked. With decades of hands-on experience, John had developed a reputation for prioritizing deadlines and efficiency above almost all else—an approach that, in his case, placed minimal emphasis on workers' safety.

Witnessing the profound impact of Eugene's leadership style, John found himself questioning the deeply ingrained tenets that had shaped his career. Confronted by the stark contrast between Eugene's empathy-driven, safety-oriented approach and his own hard-driving, results-focused mindset, John embarked on a journey of self-reflection. This process ultimately spurred him to discard his long-established attitudes in favor of a more compassionate, worker-centered philosophy.

John's transformation marked the beginning of a ripple effect that would continue to reverberate throughout the entire organization. Managers at all levels began to recognize the inherent value in adopting Eugene's approach, gradually incorporating a more empathetic stance that emphasized safety and collaboration.

With this newfound focus on human connection and team spirit, the work environment flourished. What was once a fiercely competitive, high-stress workplace gradually transformed into a harmonious, mutually supportive community where workers felt valued and cared for. This overhaul of corporate culture not only led to a marked decrease in workplace accidents but also resulted in a significant increase in job satisfaction and overall employee morale.

Although the inherently humble Eugene was quick to attribute these successes to the combined efforts of the entire team, his coworkers knew that it was his unwavering persistence and dedication to his principles that had been the spark to ignite the blaze of change.

Eugene's lasting legacy was far more profound than mere statistics. His influence extended beyond the obvious improvements in safety and well-being to encompass the very fabric of the organization, changing its culture at its deepest level. By showing his peers—both on and off the construction site—that leadership could be rooted in empathy, kindness, and a genuine concern for others, Eugene challenged conventional notions of managerial prowess and demonstrated the power of living by one's convictions.

Through his actions, Eugene proved that

leadership is not solely based on an official title or the exercise of raw authority. Instead, it can arise spontaneously from the choices and behaviors of an individual who is committed to making a tangible difference in their environment. Even a seemingly ordinary construction worker such as Eugene can embody the spirit of leadership, transforming an entire organization through their dedication and adherence to their principles.

Eugene's story stands as a shining example of how simple principles and silent leadership can have a profound, lasting impact on an organization. It offers a glimpse into the inherent power that each person holds to make a difference in the world—a power that, when exercised with care and compassion, can create ripples of change that reach far beyond the individual's immediate circle of influence. In Eugene's case, those ripples extended to his coworkers, the company's management, and, ultimately, the very heart of the construction industry as a whole. The quiet leadership of one humble worker demonstrated that transformational change, growth, and empathy are possible even amid the tumultuous cacophony of construction, proving that the true measure of a leader lies not in their designated title, but in the values, they choose to embody and the impact they have on those around them.

The Gentle Ripples of Change

Perched high in his contemporary office above New York City's bustling streets, Walter "Walt" Gray, CEO of Gray Construction Inc., felt the weight of the world bearing down on him. Each day, he faced mounting pressure to grow the company, expand its reach, and continue to satisfy shareholders while juggling a complex web of budgets, schedules, and clients. Though a respected and well-seasoned entrepreneur, the increasingly demanding nature of his industry added an almost tangible tension to his daily meetings.

One morning, as the city's skyline slowly rose from its slumber, inevitable clouds of uncertainty lingered over yet another board meeting. Reports of workplace accidents, declining moral, and rising tension amongst the workforce had created an urgent need for change, though the specifics of what that change would entail remained frustratingly elusive. As the management team debated the merits of various initiatives, all those present found themselves uncharitably dismissive of each suggestion, a telltale sign that they were merely solutions haphazardly applied to the wrong problem.

But amidst this atmosphere of doubt and frustration, something unexpected occurred. A name, whispered quietly in the room before rapidly catching on like wildfire: Eugene. It was an unassuming name, one that had initially gone unnoticed by the higher-ups preoccupied with their stressful pursuits. However, as stories of Eugene's courage, dedication, and selflessness trickled up through the ranks of the company, his quiet leadership began to demand the attention of even the most disinterested executives.

Intrigued by the almost-mythical tales of this ordinary construction worker's extraordinary acts, Walt decided to delve deeper into the world of Eugene. Hidden beneath the hard hat and yellow safety vest was a humble man whose simple principles quietly guided each of his actions. Eugene's kind, empathetic approach and unwavering commitment to the safety of his coworkers on the construction site had generated a small but powerful revolution, one that had significantly changed the dynamics of the teams he worked with and had begun to pique the interest of those higher in command.

Keenly aware of the potential value that this silent leader could bring to his struggling organization, Walt opted for a more hands-on approach. He made the unusual decision to don a disguise—a hat, sunglasses, and the loose, well-worn clothes typical of a construction worker—to observe the unassuming Eugene in his element, free from the trappings of being the CEO.

As Walt stepped onto the construction site, he

instantly felt the weight of his lofty title slip from his shoulders. He was now a nondescript observer, able to witness firsthand the remarkable impact Eugene had on his fellow workers. He watched as Eugene began each day with meticulous safety checks, fostering a sense of camaraderie among the team as he patiently instructed others on how best to prevent accidents, respect protocols, and put safety first.

Though no one had been explicitly informed that Walt was on site observing, it was not long before whispers of the CEO's curiosity began to work their way through the construction crew. The unspoken potential impact of these whispers was not lost on Eugene, who became more determined than ever to set an exemplary example for his coworkers.

As the days passed, Walt began to see the true power of Eugene's quiet leadership. The gentle giant's subtle teachings had a profound effect on the attitudes and actions of the entire team, from the most junior laborer to the most senior foreman. Walt caught a glimpse of the underlying thread that tied together the scattered stories of Eugene's humble acts and realized that it was not just his actions alone but the sweeping culture shift that had been sparked by Eugene's unwavering commitment to his principles.

Undeniably moved by what he had observed,

Walt experienced a moment of clarity. He understood that the key to resolving his organization's challenges lay not in a series of hastily conceived initiatives, but in replicating the empathetic, safety-first approach that Eugene had effortlessly instilled in his peers. Inspired by how the seemingly insignificant actions of one individual could create such meaningful change, Walt resolved to spearhead an organizational revolution—one that would not only address the industry's pressing safety concerns but also lay the foundation for a healthier, happier work environment.

Returning to the boardroom, Walt shared his findings with his management team, detailing the extraordinary impact that Eugene's quiet leadership had on both the morale and safety of the construction site. He made the case for launching a company-wide initiative to replicate Eugene's principles and foster a more empathetic work culture, one that valued teamwork and placed a premium on safety and the well-being of all employees.

Emboldened by Walt's newfound conviction, the entire management team threw their support behind the idea. Together, they worked tirelessly to develop the "Eugene Initiative," a comprehensive organizational overhaul designed to redefine the company's values and goals, placing a strong emphasis on empathy, teamwork, and safety.

The Eugene Initiative was rolled out in stages, beginning with a series of roundtable discussions to gather feedback, ideas, and suggestions from employees across the spectrum. The goal was to build a collective vision for the organization grounded in real-life experiences and knowledge, with the hope that this grassroots approach would foster buy-in from everyone involved.

The full framework of the initiative was carefully crafted and comprised various components such as revised safety protocols, ongoing training and workshops, and even quarterly employee recognition programs to celebrate everyday heroes like Eugene who went above and beyond to promote a culture of safety, empathy, and teamwork.

As the Eugene Initiative took shape, another key piece of the puzzle emerged. Walt realized that, in order to genuinely alter his organization's culture, he and his fellow executives needed to embrace Eugene's principles personally. Following an intensive self-reflective process, they grew committed to the cause, transforming their own approaches and attitudes. As a result, executive management began to prioritize empathy and employee well-being in every decision they made.

As the foundation of the new organizational culture solidified, the seemingly subtle revolution sparked by Eugene began to cause ripples throughout every level of the company. Workers felt reborn within this brand-new environment, one that encouraged collaboration over cutthroat competition. They felt valued, respected, and deeply committed to each other's safety and well-being, as well as the organization's overarching cause.

With time, the fruits of Eugene's labor became evident, as significant reductions in workplace accidents were recorded alongside a remarkably enhanced employee morale. Productivity steadily improved, as workers felt more invested in their roles, knowing that their organization genuinely cared for their welfare. The increased trust, commitment, and loyalty that resulted from this transformation had an undeniably positive impact on the bottom line.

The success of the Eugene Initiative reached far beyond the confines of Gray Construction, Inc. Other companies in the industry began to take notice and follow suit, adopting similar approaches in their own businesses as word spread about the profound effect of Eugene's quiet leadership. This humble construction worker's unwavering belief in safety, empathy, and teamwork had not only transformed a single organization but also inspired an industry-wide movement.

Years after launching the Eugene Initiative, Gray Construction, Inc. continued to thrive under the guidance of its revitalized organizational culture. The company became a beacon of hope in an industry fraught with danger, setting an example for others to follow. This sweeping change was due in no small part to the courage and conviction of Eugene, who had unwittingly sparked a revolution that would have a lasting impact far beyond the confines of his daily life.

The story of Eugene's silent leadership serves as a potent reminder that the most profound change is often born from small, unassuming beginnings. A seemingly insignificant construction worker, Eugene demonstrated that actions truly do speak louder than words and that even the smallest gestures, when performed with consistency and dedication, can leave a powerful impression on those with the power to effect change.

The transformation within Gray Construction, Inc. seemed like nothing short of a miracle. Onlookers marveled at the dramatic turnaround of a company that had been grappling with mounting safety concerns and waning employee morale just a short time prior. The success of the Eugene Initiative had not only turned the organization's fortunes, but it had also fueled a sense of renewed optimism, of pride, and of community within the workforce.

However, the effects of Eugene's quiet leadership were far from limited to his own industry. As the CEO, Walt held a prominent position within various professional circles, many of which reached far beyond the construction industry. Captivated by the power of the quiet leadership that had sparked such significant change, Walt felt compelled to share the lessons he had learned.

He began by sharing Eugene's story and the resulting cultural shift within his own company with various industry leaders during networking and social events. His narrative - the concept of transformative power held by silent leaders among the rank and file, the impact of empathy and respect on the work environment, the prioritization of safety and well-being - struck a chord with the wider audience. As more and more dialogue unfolded around Eugene's tale and the cultural shift in Gray Construction, Inc., a greater openness to his grassroots leadership style emerged.

As a man of influence, Walt was often invited to attend or speak at leadership symposiums and corporate events. Seizing these opportunities, he shared the success story of the Eugene Initiative, highlighting how instilling empathy within their teams had led to improved safety, increased productivity, and increased employee morale within his company.

In every presentation he gave and every conversation he sparked; Walt emphasized the central role of silent leaders like Eugene in driving change. His convincing articulation of the profound organizational transformation catalyzed by prioritizing safety and empathy began to attract attention from diverse corners.

Non-profit organizations, educational bodies, healthcare establishments, and more began to recognize the tremendous potential for application within their respective domains. Eugene's principles of empathy and commitment to safety were universal, equally applicable, and potentially transformative in any industry. And so, inspired by an unlikely hero at a construction company, they began to explore how to adapt the 'Eugene Initiative' to their unique contexts.

Gradually, echoes of Eugene's principles began to skirt across various organizations. Non-profit organizations, motivated by Eugene's story, began focusing on harnessing the potential of their silent leaders. Schools and educational institutions implemented empathy training programs to cultivate a more inclusive and understanding learning environment.

Healthcare facilities saw the initiative as a beacon in their journey towards patient-centric care, with empathy and safety as their cornerstones. Even large corporations outside of the construction domain started recognizing their silent leaders and began investing more heavily in employee well-being.

The conversations around the Eugene Initiative triggered by Walt's advocacy had begun to alter the landscape of leadership and organizational culture far beyond their initial scope.

By bringing Eugene's story to light, Walt effectively started a wave of cultural change that spread through various organizations, industries, and sectors. The power of the humble construction worker's silent leadership, his unwavering dedication to empathy and safety-first approach, served as a universal call to action, transcending industry-specific barriers.

As more organizations began to infuse their cultures with Eugene's values, the ripple effects became more pronounced. Reports emerged of lowered workplace conflicts, enhanced morale, increased productivity, and most notably, a resurrected faith in leadership.

Eugene's story had reached far beyond his own life, his own team, his own company, and even his own industry. This silent leader's approach to work had become a symbol, a rallying point from which organizations drew inspiration to reshape their cultures and redefine leadership in their unique contexts.

Eugene's principles, shared by Walt, sowed the seeds of change far and wide. The conversation that started in a construction company's boardroom ended up changing the way organizations globally approached leadership, proving the lasting potency of Eugene's silent leadership.

Eugene, a humble construction worker, had inadvertently left an indelible mark on the corporate world, a legacy carried forward by those willing to listen, learn, and pioneer a movement toward a more empathetic, safety-centric workplace. It was undeniably a testament to how, sometimes, the most potent lessons come not from the loud broadcast of directives from the top tiers of a company, but from the quiet, consistent actions of an individual on the ground.

Analyzing the Gentle Giant

In the grand scheme of traditional leadership models, a construction worker named Eugene serves as an unlikely protagonist. However, within his story lies an impactful narrative that showcases an alternative leadership paradigm where expression is drawn more from quiet action and dedication than from verbal rhetoric.

Arguably, Eugene's greatest offering to the concept of leadership was his embodiment of quiet consistency. Within the tumultuous environment of Gray Construction, Eugene was a beacon of stability, displaying an unwavering commitment to his role and values. Devoid of grandiose declarations or authoritative commands, his leadership was deeply embedded in his actions.

Operating in a high-risk construction environment, Eugene's leadership rested on his unwavering commitment to safety. Rather than merely professing the importance of safety, he consistently demonstrated it, adding credibility to his beliefs. In doing so, he subtly communicated the importance of a safety-first approach to his colleagues.

Why is this consistency important in leadership? The answer lies in the psychological construct of 'predictability.' When a leader, like Eugene, consistently demonstrates specific behaviors or attitudes, it minimizes ambiguity, enhancing understanding and cooperation among team members. By embracing predictable actions and attitudes – in Eugene's case, prioritizing safety – leaders can foster trust and a sense of security within their teams.

Beyond his commitment to safety, Eugene's leadership style was characterized by another potent yet often overlooked element: empathy. Instead of reprimanding his coworkers for their safety missteps, he approached them with understanding, empathy, and guidance.

In doing so, Eugene established a profound connection with his coworkers. They felt respected, valued, and understood, contributing to a deeper sense of trust and collaboration within the team. This approach also gave his colleagues the confidence to trust in Eugene's leadership, knowing that their vulnerabilities would not be used against them.

Empathy as a leadership trait cannot be overstated. Today, leaders grapple with creating enthusiastic, cohesive, and loyal teams. But how can this be achieved? The answer may lie in the exercise of empathy. By understanding and acknowledging their team members' perspectives and feelings, leaders can create a deeply supportive space that motivates and engages.

By integrating empathy into his daily interactions, Eugene built a collaborative environment rooted in respect. This approach not only catalyzed an uptick in morale and teamwork but was instrumental in creating an atmosphere receptive to change – the shift towards safer work practices.

Eugene persisted in his focus on safety, regardless of the obstructions he faced. This tenacity, an unwavering focus on his values, created a lasting impact on his coworkers. Over time, they began to realize the importance of safety, leading to a silent revolution focused on creating a safer work environment.

Eugene, in aligning his actions with his values and encouraging his peers to do the same, was displaying traits of transformational leadership. Transformational leaders inspire and motivate team members to transcend their individual interests for the greater good of the team. Eugene, with his consistent focus on safety, accentuated the need for change and, in doing so, motivated his peers to follow suit.

The influence of Eugene's leadership did not stay confined within his immediate team; it fanned out across broader circles. His principles of consistency, empathy, and safety, while embedded within a construction context, were easily adaptable - these are universally beneficial traits that find resonance across diverse environments.

The churning effect of Eugene's principles within Gray Construction was evident to everyone, even the CEO, who was moving in wider circles, where such success stories were a rarity. The compelling turnaround painted a tantalizing picture and as Walt shared the Eugene tale, it resonated with a larger audience.

Eugene's principles transcended the individual and influenced the organization at large. But it was not the person of Eugene that was scalable but the principles he embodied. The universality of these principles allowed them to be molded to fit the needs of any organization or industry, hence creating a far-reaching impact.

The aftereffects of the Eugene Initiative serve to highlight the need to integrate elements of his leadership style into contemporary practices.

The consistency shown by Eugene established him as a reliable figure within Gray Construction. Leaders must understand the power of consistency—it is not loud declarations that make an impact, but the constant, visible alignment of words and actions that engender respect and trust.

Eugene's empathetic approach towards his peers' safety mishaps played a pivotal role in forming a cohesive workforce. Empathy allows leaders to understand their team's perspective, create an inclusive environment, and foster closer connections.

The commitment that Eugene showed towards safety was a catalyst for the cultural shift in Gray Construction. A leader's commitment to their values can significantly influence an organization's culture.

Eugene effectively demonstrated the power of leading through action. He didn't instruct his co-workers to adapt safer work practices; he led them there through his behavior. This behavioral demonstration can be powerful persuaders in causing change and inspiring emulation.

Leadership isn't about the position one holds but how one influences others. A leader isn't the one who talks most loudly but the one who inspires others through action. It's crucial for leadership to recognize this and cultivate a climate where every member feels empowered to lead, initiate change, and make a difference.

Eugene's story shows that change does not have to be grand or dramatic. Sometimes, subtle, consistent actions—like emphasizing safety in day-to-day routines—can start a domino effect that can cause profound change.

Through living his values, Eugene left an imprint on the canvas of leadership that was both deep and expansive. His story underlines the critical importance of attributes like empathy, consistency, and leading by example—illustrating to leaders across the world that potent leadership can often stem from quiet, consistent action. A tale such as Eugene's defies conventional wisdom to demonstrate beautifully how humility combined with perseverance, empathy, and commitment can coalesce into a powerful leadership trajectory that has the power to effect far-reaching change.

THE CHEERFUL CUSTODIAN

T here is an unspoken quality that defines true leadership, one that transcends hierarchies and job titles. It breathes effortlessly amidst those who embrace kindness and empathy, optimism and enthusiasm. This wistful quality has the power to stir hearts and inspire lives. For the students at Pinnacle College, this elusive yet transformative power found life in a simple custodian named Eddie.

Eddie was a middle-aged custodian who had been working at Pinnacle College for over ten years. Those who meandered through the college's hallways could spot him tending to the concrete, steel, and glass that made up the campus.

While it was Eddie's job to ensure cleanliness, orderliness, and hygiene, it was his unwavering positive attitude that made the real difference. An empathetic soul in a blue-collar uniform, Eddie uplifted everyone who crossed his path – students, staff, and faculty alike. He always wore a smile on his face, a beacon of light that illuminated the dimly lit hallways, offering tired and weary students a moment of solace.

It wasn't just the shiny floors and polished doorknobs that bore testament to Eddie's meticulous attention to detail. No – Eddie approached his work with unflinching dedication, never deterred by the nature of his job or the disregard many showed towards it. Through his disarming, genuine optimism, Eddie embodied the belief that the value of one's work revolves around one's commitment, rather than its subject matter.

While many could have plummeted into bitterness, Eddie chose to rise above by forging meaning in the simplest acts of kindness. To him, wiping away a stain on the wall or picking up stray trash was as essential as unburdening the hearts of those he met. His relentless enthusiasm, deeply rooted in the joy of interacting with people, transformed his seemingly monotonous job into a conduit for positive change.

Eddie's warmth extended beyond the smiles that followed his path. He knew that higher education wasn't just an intellectual journey but also an emotional one, characterized by highs and lows. Eddie often heard the students ruminating about their academic future, classified under the strain of exams, and yet, despite it all, striving to make a difference in their world.

Time and time again, Eddie saw them with heads bowed low in resignation. But instead of lamenting their plight, he chose to sow seeds of positivity through simple conversations. He lent a listening ear and offered gentle, comforting words – small but powerful acts of kindness that reminded students that they were not alone.

These spontaneous connections brought about transformations, weaving hope and inspiration that encapsulated the essence of the college.

Such was the case of a young woman, Krista, always buried in a book. The brightness that once resided in her eyes had faded into worry. Engulfed by the fear of losing her scholarship, she spent every waking moment wringing her hands and poring over her textbooks. An overwhelming sense of panic left her feeling cold and alone.

One day, as she sat in the dim corridor with tears streaming down her cheeks, Eddie approached her with a reassuring smile and handed her a cup of hot chocolate. With the gentle guidance of a practiced listener, Eddie helped Krista to unravel the web of anxieties she had become trapped in. The conversation that ensued – one of understanding, care, and encouragement – sparked a newfound sense of courage in Krista's heart, propelling her to bravely face the turbulent days that lay ahead.

Eddie had given her the gift of belief – in herself and her potential. And beyond that, Krista's meeting with Eddie led her to understand the importance of extending warmth and kindness to others. She went on to create a peer support group for students grappling with immense academic pressure and self-doubt, instilling in them the same hope that Eddie had nurtured within her. The flame of Eddie's positive leadership had ignited the fires in her heart and, in doing so, set ablaze the hearts of others.

Then there was Keith, who originated from a small town, far away from the college's bustling campus. Struggling to adapt to the fast-paced city life while battling homesickness, he found himself teetering on the brink of isolation. Loneliness had weaved its way into his chest, tightening its grip with each passing day.

One evening, as Keith trudged through the labyrinthine corridors, Eddie offered to show him around the campus. As they wandered along the topsy-turvy passageways, Eddie shared stories of other students who had overcome similar challenges. Through his stories, Eddie breathed life into the seemingly lifeless corners of the campus – painting a vivid portrait of struggle, resilience, and hope.

In a few short hours, Eddie had peeled back the layers of the college, revealing a world of camaraderie and shared experiences. As Keith walked away, he realized that the college was now a little less unfamiliar, a little more alive – and that, suddenly, he felt a part of it. By introducing Keith to the invisible threads that connect one heart to another, Eddie had made possible the realization that he wasn't alone in his fight.

Subsequently, Keith was inspired to pledge his time to volunteering at local community events, seeking to pay forward the sense of connection and belonging he'd experienced with Eddie. In doing so, he found his life's purpose and dedicated himself to helping others find theirs, kickstarting a virtuous cycle.

Each brief encounter, every shared smile or kind word, deepened Eddie's impact on campus. The students, inspired by Eddie's enthusiasm and dedication, began to commit fervently to their work and saw school as more than a race for grades.

An alchemy of hope, joy, and inspiration permeated the college's walls, demonstrating that true leadership is not solely about the realm of executive power or corporate prowess. Eddie's actions awakened the latent potential for leadership that lies within every act of kindness, every word of encouragement, and every empathetic embrace.

The quiet, extraordinary leadership journey of Eddie the custodian offers a wealth of lessons for today's leaders. Firstly, it showcases the possibility of transforming even the most mundane tasks into purposeful and meaningful experiences.

Secondly, it highlights the importance of tuning into the emotional landscape of our surroundings; we must ourselves rise above the challenges of empathy and remain open to the needs of others. By fostering a culture of openness and kindness, today's leaders can carve out a better tomorrow for all.

Lastly, Eddie's life is a testament to the potent influence of positive leadership. He demonstrated the sublime capacity to open hearts, break down barriers, and create lasting change through small gestures of kindness and courage. To lead, we must embrace the reality that leadership starts with the simplest of encounters, the quietest of words, the most modest of jobs.

And so, as the sun sets and the echoes of laughter recede into the hallways, the name 'Eddie' may one day fade from memory. Yet, his ideals – his unwavering optimism, genuine kindness, and unassuming leadership – will continue to reverberate throughout the campus, etching themselves into the hearts of those he touched – and inspiring a new generation of leaders to forge their paths with the echoes of his gentle wisdom.

The Paradox of Pinnacle

Once a bustling hub of intellectual exploration, Pinnacle College lay nestled in the heart of the city, brimming with young minds eagerly seeking wisdom and guidance. One such guiding light was Professor Layla Henderson, a prodigious scholar who dedicated her life to the pursuit of knowledge and an influential instructor in the institution's English department.

Amid the passionate exchange of ideas and fervent scholarly pursuits, an unlikely figure stood in the backdrop: a middle-aged custodian named Eddie. Living in a world largely unnoticed, Eddie moved mindfully in the stillness, diligently cleaning hallways and classrooms and radiating an infectious, warm smile that reached every corner of the college.

Eddie intrigued Layla. His job, typically appealing to fewer people due to its demanding nature, was approached by Eddie with an unwavering spirit of acceptance and love. Layla observed Eddie in awe, often watching him traversing through the halls, carrying trash bins and mop buckets, seemingly light-hearted and enthused despite the monotonous nature of his day-to-day tasks.

Eddie displayed a rare trait that few possess: a sense of cheerfulness and contentment in an occupation that was generally undervalued and overlooked. His demeanor piqued Layla's curious nature, and she found herself meticulously noting Eddie's dedication and optimistic attitude.

To Layla, Eddie was a conundrum that needed decoding. As she began paying closer attention to Eddie's activities and interactions, she noticed a pattern that was highly peculiar for somebody in his position. During his routine chores, Eddie engaged everyone on a personal level. From faculty members to students, Eddie spared no one his contagious joy and genuine enthusiasm.

The warmth that Eddie exuded was much more than that of a well-wishing acquaintance. Eddie's attention went beyond that. From offering encouraging words to a distressed student to sharing a cup of hot chocolate with a tired faculty member during the late hours of the evening, Eddie's understanding and supportive demeanor became his distinguishing trait.

Eddie led without a title, something that surprisingly reverberated throughout the college. His humble acts of kindness and wisdom subtly bubbled around him, transforming the atmosphere at the college.

Pinnacle College had clearly outlined hierarchy

roles. Layla was used to leaders sitting in their offices strategizing, planning, and making significant decisions. However, Eddie, an individual who professionally had little chance of ascending the corporate ladder, taught her important lessons in leadership, uprooting her current perceptions.

In Eddie, Layla saw the quintessence of servant leadership — he dedicated himself to serving others through his role and actions. He practiced empathetic listening, practiced foresight, and nurtured community spirit effortlessly. Yet, Eddie's most striking quality was his ability to perceive, consider, and alleviate the emotional turbulence of individuals at the college.

The striking contrast of their roles got Layla thinking. Was she, as an esteemed academic, doing enough to ease the intellectual and emotional burdens of her students? Was she embodying the qualities of leadership in a way that would inspire her students?

Armed with her new insight, Layla began incorporating Eddie's traits into her teaching methodology. She started by honing her listening skills, giving her students the space to express their fears and hopes both about their academic life and their personal spheres.

Layla encouraged freedom of thought, encouraged her students to share their viewpoints, even if they diverged from her own lessons. She embraced the diversity of intellect and a multiplicity of perspectives, adding texture to the education she imparted.

Layla's class environment changed; they became safe spaces for intellectual and emotional exploration, akin to the warm aura that one naturally associates with Eddie. She began to understand that teaching wasn't just about relaying knowledge; it also held the transformative power to mold young minds, coaxing them not just towards qualifications but towards being better human beings.

Her syllabus started incorporating themes of empathy, altruism, and transformational leadership. Layla found herself encouraging students in a way she hadn't done before, rehashing the importance of soft skills and lifelong learning alongside hard knowledge.

Eddie's influence didn't just end at changing Layla's teaching methodology. With time, she grew to admire his ability to not chase titles or power, but seemingly derive joy from the act of service itself. In that, she saw an inspiring dichotomy — a way of uplifting oneself by uplifting others.

Recognizing the essence of his leadership, she started vocalizing his legacy, sharing Eddie's traits with her students. She explained to them the power of simple acts of kindness and dedication hold and how being in a position of power isn't the only way to lead.

Through her new approach, Layla not only enriched the minds of her students, but she also amplified Eddie's philosophy — making the world a better place one interaction at a time.

In Eddie, Layla found more than just an unexpected beacon of leadership; she found a will to adapt, a power to inspire, and the strength to transform perspectives. Eddie, the unassuming custodian, had managed to make profound ripples without the authority or hierarchy traditionally associated with leadership.

Their story is a testament to the potential that lies within each of us to shape and influence the lives around us. It doesn't matter if you're a distinguished professor or a humble custodian. What matters is the ability to harness empathy and love, exuding a spirit of service that uplifts everyone who comes across your path.

Through Eddie's legacy and Layla's transformation, the message rings clear for Pinnacle College and beyond: true leadership can breathe life in the humblest tasks and inspire the most crucial transformations. And often, it's those who are least likely to climb the corporate ladder who end up teaching us the most valuable leadership lessons. For it's not the job, but the person doing the job, that makes the real difference.

Analyzing the Cheerful Custodian

In every organizational sphere, leadership is often associated with prominent positions or powerful titles. However, solid leadership can emerge from the most unlikely sources and does not always correspond with hierarchical systems. Set within the educational echelons of Pinnacle College, an unassuming tale of leadership unfolds. It's the tale of two disparate characters —Eddie, the diligent custodian, and Layla, a passionate professor. Despite their roles being miles apart, they crafted a leadership story that left a profound, lasting impact on the whole community. In this analysis, we will delve into the unique leadership styles, traits, and attributes of Eddie and Layla, examining how their actions influenced others and the broader community. This exploration aims to unearth insights that will reshape conventional perspectives on leadership.

Illustrating an unconventional yet profoundly effective form of leadership, Eddie is a prime embodiment of Servant Leadership—a style characterized predominantly by a leader's focus on serving others above all else. This style of leadership inspires trust and loyalty among those served, ultimately fostering an environment where they feel valued and appreciated.

The Servant Leadership style is distinctly evident in Eddie's daily interactions. Despite operating in a role typically undervalued and overlooked, Eddie rendered his services with unwavering commitment, cheerfulness, and kindness. This careful attention towards even the most seemingly mundane tasks fostered a sense of worth for the otherwise invisible tasks.

On a broader scale, Eddie didn't just carry out his custodial duties efficiently; he touched lives with his warmth, empathy, and positivity. Examples from the story such as offering a consoling word to a distressed student or sharing a late-night hot chocolate with a tired faculty member highlight a leader who serves with compassion. The outcome? A significant affirmation of the effectiveness of Servant Leadership and a positive shift in the college atmosphere, leading to increased morale and a sense of belonging among the college community members.

Layla's case presents an intriguing twist to leadership. At the outset, she embodied traits common to academic leaders—intellectual savvy, high standards for achievement, and a zealous passion for her subject. However, the influence of Eddie's leadership introduced a paradigm shift in Layla's approach to her role.

Layla's traits of open-mindedness, compassion, and adaptability stood out as she internalized and mirrored Eddie's ethos in her own leadership style. Her leadership journey showcased a transformation from being primarily an intellectual guide to becoming a mentor who recognized and nurtured the holistic growth of her students.

In essence, Layla incorporated transformational leadership attributes into her style. She began to foster emotional intelligence, encouraged participation, respected diverse opinions, and diligently worked towards building a nurturing classroom environment that echoed the empathy she saw in Eddie. This adaptation was not only remarkable but also demonstrated the dynamic nature of effective leadership.

Deep diving into the leadership traits demonstrated by Layla and Eddie, we can glean three noteworthy characteristics—empathy, adaptability, and influence.

Empathy, spearheading emotional intelligence, paved the way for honest, genuine connections. When Eddie expressed empathy towards those he interacted with, it led to emotional bonding and trust-building, characteristic traits of a healthy community. Similarly, with Layla, reconfiguring her classroom atmosphere to be more empathetic, witnessed a marked improvement in student engagement, learning outcomes, and overall satisfaction levels.

On the other hand, adaptability revealed itself most significantly in Layla's shift from a traditionally intellectual leadership approach to an emotionally inclusive, empathetic one. This adaptability signified essential leadership flexibility as she learned and evolved in response to Eddie's influence.

This influence—in the context of leadership —sits at the core of Eddie and Layla's stories. Eddie's influence stemmed from his servant leadership ethos, spreading positivity, and creating a ripple effect of goodwill throughout the college. On the other hand, having internalized Eddie's philosophy, Layla's influence extended to her students' thought processes, where she successfully made the transition from imparting knowledge for grades to learning lessons for life.

Eddie and Layla harnessed different pathways in their journey as leaders. Eddie, an unassuming custodian, demonstrated impactful leadership without traditional authority. Layla, on the other hand, already held an established leadership role as a professor. However, she evolved to adopt Eddie's relatable, influence-centric leadership style.

Eddie's influence resulting from his servant leadership style lay in its 'grass-roots' accessibility. His ability to inspire and uplift without seeking power or authority demonstrated that true leadership roots from action, attitude, and the ability to bring about positive change, regardless of title or position.

On the contrary, Layla's strength stemmed from her ability to adapt and evolve her leadership to match the needs of her students. By internalizing Eddie's philosophy and modifying her teaching approach, she managed to hold a positive influence over her students, fulfilling the role of a true leader.

Despite the contrast, both styles of leadership were equally effective in engaging, connecting, and establishing a safe space where individuals could thrive, grow, and feel valued.

Gleaning insights from the leadership styles, traits, and attributes of Eddie and Layla offers us valuable lessons about leadership. Leadership is not confined to a position, power, or title, nor is it static or unchanging. Leadership is dynamic, evolutionary, and most importantly, accessible to all, regardless of the role or task at hand.

Eddie and Layla's story serves as a reminder that leadership echoes most significantly through actions, interactions, and the pursuit to uplift others—not just oneself. Through their roles and actions, they inspired those around them, allowing people to connect, grow, and thrive.

In essence, leadership can emanate from

anywhere. All it takes is an empathetic disposition, a willing heart, and an attitude of unceasing service to others, as brilliantly demonstrated by Eddie and Layla. This exploration underlines the importance of analyzing leadership characteristics, providing insights into building stronger leaders, and installing effective leadership practices in our personal and professional lives. Their story imbues hope for every individual striving for a greater purpose—a testament to the fact that any act, no matter how small it may seem, holds the potential to spark a significant change.

THE REAL ESTATE ANCHOR

Set against the vibrant backdrop of fast-paced, ever-changing cities, amidst the inviting tranquility of charming suburbs, and within the demands and dreams of potential homeowners, exists an inspiring tale. This tale serves as a guiding light, radiating a beacon of hope for those aspirants embarking on their voyage in the real estate market. This remarkable testimonial belongs to Kristen, a formidable figure standing tall and steadfast amidst the tumultuous seas of the real estate world. The story of Kristen is not a tale confined to cold facts, numbers, voluminous contracts or high-profile deals, but rather a powerful testimony to the persuasive might of ethical conduct and professionalism within the often complex and disorienting labyrinth of the real estate industry.

Kristen's story commences with her as a dynamic woman, an entrepreneur embodying determination and resilience, launching herself into the roaring whitewaters of real estate. As she deftly navigated the relentless waves, she grappled with the chatter of silver-tongued sales representatives, the pressing weight of formidable deadlines, and the seemingly endless labyrinth of paperwork and regulation. With attuned promptitude, Kristen began to understand the complex webs of the industry, developing an understanding that went far beyond the surface-level vistas of property dealings and examined the very roots of the system.

The element that discernibly set her apart, that indeed marked her out amongst the plethora of individuals navigating the same seas, was not merely her diligence, her shrewd acumen in identifying profitable ventures, or her dogged tenacity. It was rooted in her inherent commitment to two pivotal principles —professionalism and ethical conduct. These principles formed Kristen's guiding beacon, the lighthouse illuminating her path through even the stormiest of squalls and gales.

Equipped with an astute understanding of the real estate industry, Kristen slowly came to discern the ugly underbelly often veiled beneath the allure of promised wealth. She became aware of the nefarious practices that lurked beneath the placid surface and threatened to pull off course anyone navigating these paradoxical waters. The enticing whispers of exorbitant commissions held within the clasping tendrils of oral agreements, the bloated tales of property conditions stretched beyond their honest scope, the surreptitious withholding of vital information —the true DNA of the property—each of these formed the insidious traps lying in wait for the unwary navigator. The essential knowledge of these common malpractices sparked awareness in Kristen, transformed her understanding of the industry's bullish waves, and prepared her to push back against the unethical temptations that seemed to sing their fateful siren songs.

One afternoon, in the peaceful suburbs radiating dormant potential, Kristen found herself at a picturesque residential property on a warm summer day. This potential sale was requested through Mr. Bridges, a well-known figure in the suburban network of homeowners.

Mr. Bridges, completely at ease in the generously proportioned house, met Kristen with a facade of friendliness that scarcely veiled his disingenuous intent. Kristen's adept instinct, honed over countless interactions, noticed the evasive glint darting behind his seemingly ingenuous gaze. Yet, she acknowledged his welcome with a friendly nod, steadfast on preserving her professional decorum.

The home, a beautiful blend of old-world charm and modern luxury, appeared an exceptional bargain at the price Mr. Bridges had in mind. Kristen, despite the enchanting allure of the residence, felt an undercurrent of uncertainty ripple through her professional intuition. Subtle signs of discrepancy, which would have easily escaped an untrained eye, caught Kristen's attention. A slight mildew odor flowed among the household, certain wall patches that were freshly painted and didn't quite match, and a concerning absence of any past maintenance records became glaring anomalies to her seasoned scrutiny.

Discussing her concerns with Mr. Bridges about the irregularities, and requesting the absent prior maintenance records, was met with casual trivialization. He laughed it off, claiming the house was 'just old and had character', expecting Kristen to gloss over these discrepancies.

This interaction was a defining moment for Kristen. Despite standing on hardwood floors that promised comfortable remuneration, the essence of ethics could not be compromised. With an air of respectful assertiveness, she calmly informed Mr. Bridges that an honest disclosure of all potential issues was non-negotiable. And unless he agreed to this transparency, she would not represent his property.

Mr. Bridges reacted with a blend of surprise and resentment. His warning that she would regret losing this opportunity didn't deter Kristen, who remained undeterred in her principled stance. She walked away from the charming house, her character unscathed and her values unshaken.

The news about Kristen's refusal of the vintage property quietly disseminated across the suburban real estate community. Each relay of the story cemented Kristen's image as a figurehead of integrity.

As time passed, Mr. Bridges, burdened with his unsold property, attempted to engage other real estate agents, presenting the same tempting proposal.

However, these agents learned about Kristen's principled stand and its profound implications. One by one, each agent declined Mr. Bridges' listing, choosing to preserve their professional integrity over a transient financial prospect.

The true measure of an individual's character often shines brightest in turmoil. This was aptly manifested in Kristen's journey, where she unfalteringly held onto her commitment to ethical conduct and professionalism, despite the whirlpool of manipulative practices swirling around her. Kristen became an embodiment of resilience, a quality reserved for engaging leaders who inspire change and leave an indelible mark on their fields.

Her journey was marked by scrupulous efforts

to champion transparency, replacing nebulous oral dealings with clearly written contracts that upheld the values of honest trade. She championed true representation, refusing to dress properties in a deceptive guise, ensuring instead that each real estate entity she presented was portrayed in its authentic light—an honest picture, unembellished and real.

With each interaction, each meeting, Kristen exemplified the role of a real estate agent who not only advances their professional pursuits but also upholds their moral responsibility to serve their clients faithfully. As financial gains presented themselves, seductively adorned with the prospect of quick profits, Kristen's ethical compass pointed unfailingly towards customer satisfaction and their trust.

In time, Kristen's unwavering commitment to professionalism and transparency, to going beyond just performing her role as a real estate agent, began speaking volumes to her clients. Her professionalism was a silent pledge—a promise— that they were her priority, that she would always place their interests first. Despite remaining unspoken, this promise found resonance with her clientele. They began to appreciate and favor Kristen's work ethic, relishing her commitment to serve with unwavering honesty.

In the undulating sea of real estate, Kristen

emerged as an island of trust and sincerity, providing reassurance to clients worn down by deceit and foul play. In turn, the bonds of trust she established laid a solid groundwork for an escalating trajectory of customer satisfaction.

The echoes of Kristen's actions resounded beyond her business's corridors, extending into the networks of her co-workers. Slowly, their positive experiences, and subsequent implementation, began to attract a network of new clientele, paving the way for an evolving landscape of reciprocal business transactions and client referrals. Kristen's moral underpinnings, akin to the sturdy bedrock of a towering cliff, provided the platform upon which she could erect her edifice of enduring and virtuous success.

Kristen's feats not only carried her to the lofty peaks of individual success but also sowed the seeds of inspiration, sparking a revolution amidst her peers. The ripples of Kristen's ethical conduct started shaping the real estate landscape, nudging her contemporaries towards a more introspective evaluation of their practices. The undeniable benefits of her professionalism, the trust and loyalty she earned from her clients, provided tangible evidence of the merits of operating with an ethical compass.

Like a pebble dropped into a still pond, Kristen's influence created a ripple effect, prompting her peers to progressively embrace ethicality, transparency, and genuine representation in their own work. As more agents began to follow Kristen's path, adopting and implementing her principles, there dawned a slow, yet tangible transformation in the industry—an epoch that sought to mitigate the overarching storms and foster a more ethical and transparent real estate landscape.

Kristen's unwavering integrity has become the hallmark of her success in the real estate business; it is a beacon that shines brightly in a world where dishonesty and deception often lurk beneath the surface. Her steadfast commitment to ethical conduct and professionalism is not just a personal choice but an exemplary path that has inspired her peers and set new standards of excellence in the industry. By refusing to bow to the temptations of quick profits through deceitful practices, Kristen has demonstrated that integrity yields lasting success and fosters enduring relationships with clients. This steadfast moral compass instills deep trust, generating repeat business and referrals, ultimately creating a virtuous cycle of mutual gain. Her dedication to transparency, honesty, and ethical conduct has resonated with her clients and become the bedrock of her thriving business. Kristen's resolute integrity serves as a guiding light, illuminating the path to prosperity and a more ethical real estate landscape for all those inspired by her journey.

Kristen's journey signifies much more than just her laudable achievements. It's a call—an invitation—a beacon of guiding light for all those who stand at the shore, looking out towards the vast expanse of real estate waters uncertainly. Regardless of whether you're a seasoned navigator or a novice yet to find your sea legs, the principles exemplified by Kristen -- transparency, ethical conduct, and professionalism -- are lifeboats that can guide and protect you amidst the tumultuous waves.

As any leader endeavors to traverse the convoluted straits, pledge to carry forward Kristen's legacy, emulating her unwavering commitment to operate with integrity and professional conduct. Foster and nourish a successful future—one that is built on trust, mutual respect, and satisfaction. And whether the leader is about to embark on a maiden voyage or navigating the roaring waters, always remember these wise words – every rewarding journey begins with a single step of courage towards the sea.

A Lighthouse of Integrity

Noah thought he found his calling, but it was a chance association as a client of Kristen's that propelled him onto an entirely different trajectory.

Noah had been a diligent sales representative,

his days saturated with sharp conversations, looming metrics, and a relentless tide of paperwork. Scouting and transacting deals was his field of play, having developed an intimate understanding of the trade's intricate weave. But beneath the veneer of profit and transactions, Noah grappled with an unsettling observation: the insidious deceits, the pulled wool over the eyes of trusting clients.

He had begun to perceive the sinister shadows underlying the reputed glamour of the market. Its multitude of unethical practices— overblown commissions concealed within verbal agreements, amplified conditions dissolving once the acquisition was sealed, withheld factual data—offended his conscience. He yearned for transparency and honesty in an industry flooding with murky malpractices.

Enter Kristen—a competent realtor, a mariner steering her vessel through the formidable waves of the real estate ocean, guided by the lighthouse of ethical conduct and professionalism. She was a stalwart tower amid the choppy waters of deceit and clipping corners, her beacon of moral fortitude leading her way. Noah observed how Kristen swam against the strong currents of foul play, never surrendering to their relentless pull. He admired her untiring pursuit of ethical practices, how she chose integrity over the allure of unjustified commissions, and her commitment to provide customers with a frank portrayal of each property—the naked, honest truth, void of fiction.

Seeing Kristen uphold ethical standards in a largely gray landscape sowed the seeds of perception-alteration in Noah's mind. The resonance of principled business conduct amidst the cacophonous clamor of deceitful transactions sparked an inspiration. Noah began contemplating veering away from his direct sales role, sinking roots in a space where he could work to improve the market's ethical framework.

This spark of aspiration transformed into a compelling vision as Noah observed the ripple effects of Kristen's business approach. The undeniable surge in customer satisfaction, the robust trust she constructed with each client, the tangible impact on her business growth —these results spoke volumes. The fusion of ethics and transparency had proved itself a successful business strategy. Her leadership and ethical alignment had created a climate of trust, generating profitable chains of repeat business transactions and client referrals, reaffirming Noah's desire to initiate a transformation.

Fueling his ambition was his experience as a sales representative. He had navigated the stormy sea of sales, and his hands had felt the chilly touch of underhanded sales practices. Noah aspired to be the change he wished to see in the sales world.

He envisioned a business environment that didn't merely dare to dream of ethical sales strategies but made them a reality.

Observe, learn, apply—Noah resolved to set this wheel in motion for himself. Emboldened by Kristen's journey, he decided to extend her legacy—carry her torch by transitioning from a sales representative to an ethical auditor of sales practices.

Committed to his vision, Noah embarked on a transformative journey. He consumed volumes of knowledge about auditing, ethics in business, and law, seeking every possible opportunity to equip himself for his new mission. This was new terrain, unfamiliar and challenging, but Noah recognized the value of perseverance from Kristen's trajectory. His resolve hardened with each step he took towards his audacious goal. He proposed and developed ethical auditing systems aimed at encouraging transparency in sales deals and ensuring complete disclosure of vital deal-related information.

Noah's conversion into an ethical sales auditor was not an isolated endeavor. It created a harmonious symphony—slowly fostering a shift in the sales representatives' outlook towards their profession. His leadership capabilities became evident as he prioritized ethical standards over sales targets, enforcing strict auditing measures for any digression.

Companies were initially resistant, but over time, they couldn't turn a blind eye to the undeniable positive impact. A more ethical business landscape started to emerge, reflecting his robust leadership and ethical alignment mirrored by Kristen. His unwavering commitment to ethical standards encouraged others in the industry, their shared aspiration slowly but surely redefining the sales landscape.

As an ethical sales auditing mastermind, Noah encountered tremendous pressures but just like Kristen, he remained steadfast. Met with opposition and skepticism, he held on to his vision—a sales industry that doesn't compromise its ethical integrity. His consistent adherence to ethical practices awarded him the reputation of a trusted and impartial auditor. Organizations that adapted to his ethical auditing guidelines noticed a rise in customer satisfaction—just like Kristen had in her domain. A robust trust began developing with their clients, leading to a noticeable increase in repeat transactions and client referrals.

As a direct consequence of his contribution, the industry started experiencing slow yet significant changes. Sales organizations started practicing full transparency in transactions, and verbal deals turned into written agreements. The result was a noticeable shift towards ethicality—a shift toward truth and integrity.

Noah's transition from a sales representative to an ethical auditing influencer exemplifies an extraordinary journey, driven by righteous courage and an unwavering resolve to usher in a positive transformation. His actions have resonated in the realm of sales, enforcing a direction of professionalism and ethical conduct.

Noah's story is proof that leadership capabilities paired with ethical standards can contribute to better business environments, change the field of sales beyond recognition, and steer the course toward a future infused with honesty, trust, and clarity.

The journey may seem challenging, the sea choppy, yet the shore is in sight for those ready to weather the storm. Inspired by Kristen's example and drawing from his own, Noah becomes a guiding light, a beacon to sales representatives around the world, upholding the essence of ethical conduct, and proving that each one of us can make a significant change, one step at a time.

Analyzing the Real Estate Anchor

In an age where corporate scandals and misconduct frequently dominate headlines, the extraordinary tale of Kristen and Noah emerges as a beacon of ethical conduct in the business landscape. The narrative is compelling, not merely for the individuals it involves, but more importantly, for the profound lessons it imparts about the real impact of ethical leadership within organizations.

The story offers an engaging perspective, demonstrating how leaders, guided by moral values, can engender transformational change that far exceeds the bounds of their immediate surroundings and challenges conventional wisdom.

Through its real-world lens, the tale unravels the moral fabric inherent in effective leadership, highlights the significance of individual acts of integrity, and underscores their direct impact on an organization's culture, performance, and reputation.

Defining ethical leadership involves more than presenting a theoretical framework; it warrants a deeper exploration of values, actions, and consequences. Ethical leaders embody a set of principles underpinned by respect for the rights and dignity of others. These leaders don't merely tout ethical ideals - their actions demonstrate them, leading by example and steering their departments or organizations with a moral compass. Their judicious decisions aren't solely centered around profits and business gains but are guided by a considerate understanding of the ethical repercussions and a commitment to doing what is right.

The need for such ethical decision-making in leadership roles is necessary, particularly in the contemporary world fraught with multi-faceted ethical dilemmas. Leaders must navigate uncharted territories, balance conflicting interests, and make tough calls impacting multiple stakeholders.

Ethical leadership embodies multiple potent benefits for leaders themselves. It fosters a culture of credibility and trust, bolstering the leader's standing and creating a harmonious environment where employees feel genuinely valued. This culture resonates deeply with employees, leading to heightened loyalty, increased commitment, and enhanced productivity.

An ethical leader akin to Kristen, for instance, becomes a guiding light, inspiring and motivating her team through her actions, molding a set of individuals into a high-performing unit relentlessly committed to achieving organizational goals. Such ethical leadership also propels a strategic shift in cultural sensibilities. It infuses an ethos-centric approach within every organizational transaction and decision, driving mutual respect and enhancing overall team performance.

When examined from an organizational

perspective, ethical leadership presents a slew of benefits. It generates a positive organizational culture, nurturing an environment that radiates a sense of purpose that transcends profit. Ethical leaders serve a purpose that binds the employees together, a shared sense of values that inspire commitment to roles beyond contractual obligations.

Leaders like Kristen, guided by a powerful ethical compass, fortify the organization's moral framework. They promote openness and transparency, laying the foundation of a trustful climate that encourages responsible conduct from all members. Such a principled stance assists organizations in securing long-term sustainability and forging a robust reputation that serves as a competitive advantage in the increasingly value-conscious marketplace.

The harsh repercussions of unethical leadership contrast starkly with the benefits of their ethical counterparts. Unethical conduct has a cascading effect, with a plethora of damaging consequences unfurling within individuals and organizations. As revealed in Noah's initial tenure, unethical practices can erode employee morale, decrease productivity, and lead to a rapid attrition rate among valuable employees.

As a result, the work environment morphs into an unstable ecosystem riddled with doubt and mistrust. The repercussions extend beyond the confines of the organization, potentially leading to severe legal and financial penalties. It also tars the organization's reputation, breeding skepticism among consumers and stakeholders and dampening prospects of long-term success.

Applying a microscopic lens to Noah's and Kristen's leadership attributes presents a striking case study of leadership styles and their tangible impacts. Kristen, an embodiment of ethical leadership, exuded a steadfast commitment to honesty and fairness. Her actions fostered a proactive and dedicated team that became a driving force behind her organization's growth. Her firm adherence to ethical standards, reinforced by her personal integrity, built trust among her team members and clientele. The respect she earned encouraged open communication and fostered a vibrant team environment where every member felt valued and contributed enthusiastically.

On the other hand, Noah's leadership, marred initially by the presence of unethical practices, produced detrimental effects around him. His team members, anxious due to the lack of transparency and fair dealing, struggled with low morale and performed below their potential. The silver lining emerged when Noah, inspired by Kristen, emphasized ethical leadership, demonstrating the potential for change –an essential attribute of a good leader. His transformative journey showcases how promoting ethical practices can positively impact teams, boost productivity, and drive broad positive changes throughout the business ecosystem.

Noah's journey illustrates a great truth – that ethical conduct isn't a mere checklist exercise but a transformative force that can drive immense positive change. His move from being within an ethically flawed environment to becoming a champion of ethical auditing reaffirms the integral role that ethical leadership plays in organizational growth. Ethical leadership doesn't merely concern itself with achieving objectives; it meticulously considers how those objectives have been achieved.

Leaders who advocate ethical practices, like Kristen and Noah, serve as guiding lights in a landscape that often oscillates uncertainly between profit and principles. These leaders set powerful examples, weaving compelling narratives in their wake that highlight how organizations fueled by ethical conduct can indeed thrive. The tales remind us that at the juncture of business and ethics, values like integrity, honesty, and transparency aren't just morally right – they're vital for creating an empowering, productive work environment destined for success.

THE POWERLESS MANAGER

J ackson had always aspired to a leadership role in his professional journey. He worked for a prominent organization, a giant entity in the industry, where the term "Manager" was considered a badge of prestige and a symbol of profound success. Ever since he set his foot on the career ladder, Jackson had held this title in high esteem, contemplating it as the threshold of professional triumph. He believed that he, one day, deserved to be a leader, and by the virtue of this anticipated title, he thought people would, by default, follow his lead. His dreams seemed to reach fruition when he received the much-anticipated promotion to manager.

Jackson stood at the zenith of success, or so he envisioned. The chime of achievement and the stamp of a powerful title, "Manager," were resonating in his heart and mind. The weight of his career progression was undeniably exciting, like holding a priceless trophy aloft for the world to admire. However, the bubble of his elation was promptly burst when he stepped into the reality of his role that stood in stark contrast to his preconceived notions. He was a manager by designation but bereft of any significant authority.

In his initial days as a newly promoted manager, Jackson evoked little respect from his team, which became evident from multiple interactions during that period.

At a core strategy meeting, for instance, Jackson presented an exhaustive plan outlining the roadmap for their next project. He had spent hours meticulously curating the strategy, expecting an overwhelming response from his team. However, the room fell eerily silent after his presentation, with glances exchanged among the team members. A few brief, perfunctory nods were the only response he received. The lack of not only enthusiasm but even basic input from his team was staggering and quite hurtful.

On another occasion, during one of their weekly progress review meetings, Jackson attempted to address underperformance within the team and suggest ways to improve. Midway through his speech, one of the senior team members interrupted, questioning the viability of Jackson's suggestions. The concern was echoed by others in the room, leaving Jackson flabbergasted. His attempts to provide guidance and improve productivity were met with not just indifference, but also defiance.

There were countless such situations where Jackson felt a palpable disregard from his team towards his new standing. His emails often went unresponded, his feedback unacknowledged, and his attempts to foster team spirit and camaraderie largely ignored. His team seemed stuck in the past, viewing him as the same peer he was before his promotion, refusing to acknowledge his new role as their leader.

The indifference and silent rebellion from his subordinates felt like a continual blow to Jackson's newly acquired sense of authority. Everywhere he turned, he was met with veiled questioning eyes that implicitly challenged his right to lead. It was demoralizing and deeply frustrating. He had aspired and worked hard to reach this managerial position, but the reality was far from the rosy picture he had painted in his mind.

Jackson felt isolated professionally. His team's apathy made him question his abilities and self-worth, taking a toll on his confidence. As an aspiring leader, it was heartbreaking for Jackson to witness the tangible lack of trust, respect, and acceptance from his team. He was stuck in a vortex of self-doubt and frustration, acutely sensing the stark contrast between the man he wanted to be for his team and the man they viewed him as.

It was a painful realization that the title, which he believed would instantly grant him authority, respect, and compliance, was merely ornamental without the core essence of leadership.

His promotion, which was initially a cause for celebration, started feeling hollow and devoid of essence. His managerial badge shone brightly, but it did little to cast an influential light on his team's loyalty. The dissonance spurred thoughts and emotions as profound and stark as a stormy winter night. And there he stood, grappling with a perplexing question—why did the key to leadership, which he had assumed, eluded him so?

Jackson's transition was not smooth. It was a bumpy ride of realization, denial, and frustration. His journey was characterized by a profound dichotomy—his shiny title incongruously juxtaposed with his team's apathy toward his supposed authority. His dictations and strategies were met with lukewarm responses, devoid of genuine motivation. The echo of "Manager" created a void within him, a hollow chasm that seemed increasingly daunting and unbridgeable. Denial was his initial companion, a faithful attendant to this bewildering scenario.

But as denial started losing its sheen, frustration replaced it—sharp, scathing, and clouding his judgment. He felt isolated, left stranded in a position that offered him a magnificent throne but no subjects, a crown but no followers. His sense of betrayal compounded his aversion, fueling feelings of resentment toward the system that offered him leadership in name yet deprived him of the dignity and influence that should crown such a position. In Jackson's slowly spinning whirlpool of negative emotions, frustration took the leading stage.

However, amidst the fog of disillusionment, a spark of resilience ignited. His distress was slowly transforming into enlightenment, imploring him to rethink conventional leadership constructs. The frustration paved the way for a powerful realization: if a title couldn't endow you with leadership, you had to earn it through actions, commitment, and integrity. He decided to face the music and dance to its rhythm rather than remain a passive spectator.

Plunged into this profound introspection, Jackson made a vital decision—he would be a leader by example. Instead of waiting for respect to accompany his title, he chose to earn it through exemplary actions. His dedication became unwavering. His commitment deepened. He began embodying the work ethic he desired to instigate in his team, demonstrating resilience in the face of adversity, and exuding an aura of positivity to cushion the inevitable blows of negativity.

Communication and transparency became his

pivotal tools. He worked tirelessly to ensure that his team felt respected and heard. He exhibited adaptability and moldability, demonstrating that he was not a distant director but a team player, as much part of the team's successes and failures as any other team member. He listened more than he dictated, learning important lessons from feedback, promoting a culture of collective decision-making, and leading by example.

He realized the importance of honesty, responsibility, and respect in shaping true leadership, and his actions reflected these values. He made a conscious effort to lead his team not from a pedestal of power, but from a platform of shared responsibility. His actions communicated more than his words, and he became an emblem of dedication, integrity, and respect. He took on challenging tasks head-on, committed to setting a precedence for his team to emulate.

As Jackson transformed himself and his approach to leadership, he noticed a palpable shift within his team. They started mirroring his commitment and dedication, gradually aligning with his principles and strategies. Not because he demanded it, but because he had earned it. He had become more than just a "Manager." Jackson was evolving into a true leader, a beacon of inspiration, guidance, and support to his team.

During their weekly team meeting, when a

heated discussion about a challenging client was underway, Jackson stepped in not to issue orders, but to facilitate dialogue and better understanding among his teammates. His calm demeanor and genuine intent to resolve the differences without imposing his decision made his team realize the progressiveness in his leadership approach. Jackson's ability to turn heated debates into productive discussions was a stark but inspiring contrast to his initial attempts at directive leadership.

In another instance, a member of Jackson's team, Amy, was struggling with a particularly difficult element of the project. Instead of reprimanding her for the delay or assigning the task to someone else, Jackson sat down with her, explaining the components of the project and guiding her through the complexities. He worked side by side with Amy until late in the night, ensuring she felt confident enough to handle the assignment on her own. This action was a powerful testament to Jackson's commitment to mentorship and team support, and it deeply impacted the rest of the team.

Another subtle yet significant change was in the way Jackson dealt with mistakes. When Peter, a junior team member, made an error that caused a delay in project delivery, instead of rebuking him publicly, Jackson had a private conversation with him. He used the situation as a teaching moment, explaining the gravity of the error, but also emphasizing that it was an opportunity to learn and grow. Jackson's empathetic response left an indelible mark on Peter and taught the team a lesson in handling mistakes with grace and empathy.

These instances were reminiscent of the varying, yet impactful measures Jackson took to foster an environment of mutual respect, transparency, and collaboration. The more his team interacted with him, the more they experienced his evolution from a powerless manager into a true leader.

As time progressed, his team started to see a discernible shift in his leadership style – the way he communicated, how he handled conflicts, and his approach to problem-solving. Seeing Jackson walk the talk, lead by example, and respect their feedback made the team reevaluate their initial perceptions of him. His continuous striving for mutual respect, shared responsibility, and collective triumph resonated deeply with his subordinates.

Slowly, a newfound respect for Jackson began to take root within their hearts. They started trusting his decisions, respecting his insights, and valuing his opinions. His authoritative standing was no longer a subject of silent rebellion; instead, it became a badge of honor for the team. The man who once stood alone now stood strongly, but within the circle of his team, not outside it. The man they initially viewed as a peer with an undeserved higher rank was now their leader. Little by little, through his actions and commitment, Jackson had earned the respect and trust of his team. He had not just become their manager; he had become their leader.

This journey, a tumultuous adventure riddled with trials, tribulations, moments of self-doubt, and soul-stirring epiphanies, became the crucible that ultimately refined Jackson's perspective on leadership. As he battled against the tides of apathy and disappointment, he pioneered a transformative and trailblazing mindset. He discovered that the essence of authority did not lie in wielding power with an iron fist or instilling fear, but in the ability to nurture trust, to incite a sense of shared responsibility, and to cultivate an environment where mutual respect was paramount. Consequently, the gateway to collective triumph was paved. Thus, Jackson's revelation about leadership transcended the limitations of commanding and controlling; instead, he found that true leadership meant being an exemplary figure, inspiring and motivating others through actions and deeds rather than mere directives.

Jackson's odyssey from being a mere title holder—a powerless figurehead—to an influential, morally authoritative leader is a compelling illustration of the transformative potential inherent in genuine leadership. This potential lies in the foundation of actions, unwavering commitment, and rock-solid integrity, far surpassing the superficiality of lofty titles and designations. His tale serves as an invaluable lesson to all those who aspire to lead, debunking the common myth that the mere possession of a prestigious title automatically confers leadership attributes. In reality, it is an empty shell, rendered hollow and resounding in the face of true leadership. While a position of authority may indeed offer a platform or an opportunity to lead, it is not the be-all and end-all of leadership. Genuine, effective leadership is not handed over on a silver platter—it is a skill that must be scrupulously honed, nurtured, and earned through personal growth, continuous learning, and staunch dedication.

As Jackson's story teaches us, the true essence of leadership is far deeper than any title could ever convey. It is an authentic connection with others, a genuine understanding of the team's needs, and an unwavering commitment to the shared vision. Leadership, in its most effective form, requires self-awareness, humility, empathy, and the ability to adapt and grow with the team. Leadership's transformative power, when wielded ethically and responsibly, impacts not only the team but also the organization and the leader themselves.

In a world where superficiality often trumps substance, Jackson's journey offers a much-needed lesson in the distinction between holding a leadership position and being a true leader. By shedding his complacency and embracing the arduous path of self-growth and learning, Jackson became the epitome of a morally authoritative leader who inspired his team through actions, dedication, and integrity. His transformation is evidence that the essence of leadership goes far beyond fancy titles but lies in the heart of an unwavering commitment to building trust, fostering respect, and catalyzing the synergistic power of teamwork.

Jackson's experience outlines a powerful truth: leadership isn't a title, it's a responsibility. It entails creating an atmosphere of integrity, fostering a culture of trust, and nurturing an environment conducive to growth and development. It demands leading with authenticity, treating everyone with respect, and taking the journey with the team, at their pace, and in their midst. It implies learning to cheer and support, to give more, and to be, above all, a team player—because, at the end of the day, true leadership emanates not from authority but from respect and trust.

As he navigated through the trials, tribulations,

and valuable lessons that his managerial role steeped in, Jackson understood that leadership isn't a mantle that one merely puts on after ascending to a higher position—it's a way of life. A leader is an inspirational figure who manifests traits of integrity, empathy, resilience, respect, and commitment, and it is these traits that make them worthy of being followed.

In a world where leadership is often mistaken for authority, Jackson's journey offers an enlightening perspective. It reminds us all, that leadership is not about expecting subordinates to follow without question but about inspiring them to follow willingly. Through his journey of becoming a true leader by demonstrating integrity and commitment, Jackson shows that the real power of leadership lies not in the title but in influencing others positively and working together towards a shared goal. Hence, effectiveness in leadership doesn't stem from one's position alone but from how one exercises the responsibilities and obligations that accompany it.

The Coveted Role

Marcus harbored a relentless streak of ambition within him. His aspirations saw him in a glass office with a striking view from the top, shadowed by towering skyscrapers in the bustling heart of the city. He envisioned his workdays punctuated with strategic brainstorming sessions, financial analyses, client meetings, and leading a team of dedicated professionals. He imagined himself at the helm, steering the ship through turbulent market conditions, directly contributing to the future course and success of the organization.

Therefore, when Jackson, his colleague and friend from the corporate trenches, was the one promoted to that coveted managerial position, a position he firmly believed was his to claim, it was akin to a sucker punch in his gut.

Marcus was unquestionably confident in his professional skills, knowledge, and commitment. The scales of experience weighed heavier on his side, and the instances of him burning the midnight oil were countless, all adding to his perception of being more deserving. He was undeniably quick to pick up on emerging industry trends and his assertive personality commanded attention during project discussions. His proficiency at work made him believe that the managerial position was his inevitable next step.

The thought of Jackson, with his light-hearted banter and easy-going nature at the helm, seemed like a cruelly spun tale of reality. Whispers of resentment quietly began crawling into his thoughts every time he saw Jackson leading meetings, making pivotal decisions that Marcus thought were his calls to make. The seed of bitterness took root and began to distort his view of Jackson's actions and decisions.

This growing bitterness and unvoiced dissatisfaction weren't as veiled as Marcus assumed them to be. They seeped into group meetings, tainting his interactions with Jackson, becoming glaringly apparent to everyone in the team. What should have been healthy debates turned into contentious arguments; what should have been constructive critique became opportunities for sharp comebacks.

His pronounced discontent and dismissive behavior towards Jackson blared at his inability to gracefully accept the twist of fate. At this point, Marcus exhibited a lack of essential followership qualities, such as respect for leadership, openness to feedback, and commitment to team objectives over personal ones.

"Jackson, have you even considered the repercussions of this approach? We could lose our client's trust if we don't meet their expectation!" Marcus's tone dripped with condescension during one of their strategy planning meetings. His dismissive tone and disregard for Jackson's authority were pretty evident, causing an uncomfortable silence in the room - a classic example of their early confrontations.

As the weeks lengthened into months, Jackson's leadership style began to evolve in a way that Marcus hadn't anticipated. He expected Jackson's leadership style to be autocratic, brash, and impulsive due to pressure and unfamiliarity of the new role. Instead, he was met with an increasingly people-centric, self-aware, and ethical leader. Jackson was changing into a figure that sincerely cared about the people around him. He shared the responsibility of success and failure instead of taking credit for the former and pointing fingers at the latter.

Particularly memorable was an episode where a critical error by a junior team member led to a delay in project delivery. Marcus braced himself for the wrath and retribution from Jackson, much like a thunderous storm after a spell of stifling calm. However, Jackson surprised Marcus and the rest of the team with his composed response. He acknowledged the error in front of the team, yet he took it as an inadvertent, one-off mistake, focusing on how to mitigate its impact rather than penalizing the person responsible. This situation made Marcus see the humility and wisdom behind Jackson's leadership.

On a different occasion, Marcus watched as Jackson sat with Amy, who was visibly struggling with a critical component of their project. He could've easily re-allocated the task to a more experienced team member to speed things up. Instead, he opted to tutor her, spending hours discussing, explaining, and clarifying her doubts. Such instances became hallmarks of Jackson's newfound leadership style — leading by showing the path rather than directing from afar.

As such instances increasingly became the norm, Marcus's perception of Jackson and his own actions began to shift. He slowly became aware that his views had been clouded by a sense of entitlement and a misplaced perception of superiority. The resentment that had once blinded him started to erode, leaving room for introspection. He began to understand the folly in his actions and the negativity he was bringing to the team. His years of work experience had, in a way, created a barrier that kept him from seeing the critical elements of being a leader - humility, empathy, respect, and responsibility.

Marcus realized the error of his ways and committed to change. Jackson's transformation had shown him that successful leadership isn't about assertiveness and aggression, but about respect and empathy. Admitting his past mistakes became the first step in this journey. He began treating each interaction as a chance to learn, grow, and contribute positively to the team. Marcus started involving himself more proactively, not in defiant disagreement, but in collaborative problem-solving and decision making. The bitterness in his tone began to fade, replaced by a willingness to learn and to contribute positively to the discussions.

Towards the end of a Monday morning project update meeting, Marcus asked to speak. "Jackson," he began, his voice firm but respectful, "I'd like to acknowledge your management over the past few months. Some of the decisions and changes you implemented are responsible for our success in this project. I also want to apologize if I've come across as unsupportive before; I am committed to working together for our team moving forward." This was a watershed moment in their relationship, marking Marcus's transition from a disgruntled colleague to a supportive team player.

What started as resentment and rivalry gradually grew into respect. Marcus began to appreciate the value of collaboration, open communication, and mutual respect in a team setup, which Jackson effectively nurtured. His envy dramatically changed into respect for Jackson's ability to evolve as a leader. Marcus had started to learn the essence of not just being a successful leader but also a respectful follower. Growth, he realized, was not just about climbing the hierarchy but also about upliftment and development of the team he led. And Jackson, with his humility and people-centric leadership, had silently laid the foundation for this growth in Marcus.

Analyzing The Powerless Manager

The story of Jackson's progression from a fresh,

yet slightly dominant leader, to an effective and respected manager is demonstrative of the critical value of adaptability in leadership. It narrates an essential lesson about the fluidity of power dynamics and the impact a flexible management style can have on a team's overall performance and on individuals' professional growth. Initially, Jackson's management style took on an authoritarian hue. Fueled by the need to make his mark and establish his position in the team, Jackson, whether consciously or not, presented himself as a somewhat dictatorial leader, quick to make decisions without the proper consultations or team buy-in.

However, as time advanced, radical changes were made to Jackson's leadership approach - changes that became the cornerstone of the team's productivity and cohesion. Jackson evolved into a more participative leader, keenly listening to the inputs of his team members and deploying a remarkable situational leadership style. This form of leadership, characterized by the understanding that different situations call for different leadership approaches, saw Jackson evolve from a one-size-fits-all sort of leader to one who takes the time to consider the unique elements of every situation before making decisions.

Jackson also demonstrated high emotional intelligence, a crucial leadership trait necessary for fostering team unity and cohesion. Emotional intelligence was illuminated through the way Jackson managed his reactions to undue criticism and hostility, especially from Marcus. Despite Marcus's challenging attitude, Jackson was able to hold firm, showing empathy during individual interactions and deploying the required patience when resistance presented itself. Navigating through these often emotionally charged situations required an emotionally intelligent leader who could steer the ship without fostering resentment or further antagonism.

Furthermore, Jackson's humility shone through in his leadership transformation. Jackson did not take the easy way out when dealing with struggling team members. Rather than reassigning their tasks to perceived 'star' team members, he elected to provide support, aiming to help his team members develop their skills and capacity to execute their tasks effectively.

Another crucial trait Jackson exhibited was accountability. This was made evident during the incident of the project delay. Rather than taking the easy route of blaming individuals and causing acrimony among the team, Jackson elected to focus on the error itself. He publicly addressed the error, shifting the focus to the corrective measures that could be taken to rectify the error and prevent a future occurrence. These actions display Jackson not just as a leader preaching commitment to accountability, but one modeling it, setting a clear example for his team to follow.

Jackson's evolution from an authoritative to a more participative style of leadership underlined his adaptability. It showed his willingness to shift existing paradigms and adopt a fresh approach that better served the team's collective growth and goal attainment. As Jackson took on this more participative approach, he began to embed a team-oriented culture, fostering an environment where everyone felt heard, valued, and integral to the team's achievements.

Jackson's behavioral changes had a profound impact on team dynamics, leading to an improved team atmosphere. Previously dominated by resentment, tension, and conflict, the atmosphere morphed into a more collaborative one, characterized by open communication and a focus on personal growth and learning. Jackson's commitment to grow alongside his team, to learn and unlearn where necessary, resulted in a positive work environment that went beyond just pushing productivity. It created a space of unity and mutual respect, a space where individuals felt seen and valued.

An essential element of leadership effectiveness as portrayed in Jackson's story is the capacity to foster a positive team environment. This was achieved by promoting open communication, empathetic interactions, and leading by example. Adaptive leaders like Jackson mold their leadership based on their team's needs, contributing to increased productivity and greater satisfaction among team members. It exalts the value of flexibility, highlighting how adaptive leaders are better equipped to navigate team dynamics and foster greater unity in the work environment.

Parallel to Jackson's leadership journey was Marcus's transformation, which stands as a tangible testament to the significance of followership in achieving team objectives. Initially, Marcus portrayed the traits of an antagonistic follower. He constantly challenged authority and showed little cooperation with Jackson's decision-making, embodying toxic traits that posed a potential danger to the team's progress.

Despite Marcus's challenging start, his story unfolded to reveal a transformation centered on resilience and self-awareness. It was this resilience that saw Marcus moving past his bitterness and resentment and replacing it with a renewed eagerness to learn, cooperate, and contribute positively to the team's objectives.

Marcus's transformation also exposes the importance of feedback receptivity and adaptability, essential traits all followers should imbibe. Marcus learned to abandon his ego, embracing feedback and the learning opportunities they presented. He became more adaptive to the changing dynamics within the team, aligning himself more with the team's collective goals.

Marcus's transformation wasn't just about him. It also significantly eased the existing tension within the team and fueled an environment that upheld growth and learning. Marcus's newfound respect for Jackson, coupled with his drive to support the team's objectives, led to improved team dynamics and greater efficiency.

Marcus's transformation from a toxic to a supportive and respectful follower illustrates the importance of adaptive followership. It shows that the role of followers in a team is just as significant as that of the leaders. Effective and supportive followers contribute to a positive team culture, aid smoother decision-making processes, and foster overall cohesion within the team.

In conclusion, the transformational journeys of Jackson and Marcus provide cogent lessons in the critical need for adaptability in leadership and respectful followership. They underline the necessity for leaders and followers to remain agile, self-aware, respectful and humble for the overall progression of the team. They highlight the need for all team members to align with team objectives, focusing not just on individual achievements but on collective success.

By understanding the significance of adaptability, open communication, empathy, and humility in leadership and followership, team members can contribute more effectively to the overall growth and development of the group. Through the unfolding of these two transformational journeys, the story underscores the need for an environment where everyone can maximize their potential and collectively work towards achieving team success.

LEADERSHIP IN SYMPHONY

Prior to the in-depth observation of unseen leadership, if posed with the question, 'Where does leadership reside?' one might picture statistics-laden boardrooms or noise-filled political arenas. However, as we journeyed through the diverse narratives of leadership, we discovered that leadership has a wider application than traditionally perceived. Leadership embodies the essence of collective good and surfaces in the most unlikely corners of shared experiences. Its manifestation is deeply rooted in the subtlety of shared thoughts and gestures, all quietly functioning as catalysts for transformation.

Consider the motion of your life as a beautiful river. Look closely, and you'll unearth invaluable leadership pearls throughout its course. These small but significant instances of leadership are omnipresent. They can be found in an everyday conversation with a trusted mentor, in the reassuring words of a fellow traveler, or the determined voice of a construction worker tirelessly advocating for change. These seemingly 'everyday people' hold a beautiful mirror to every one of us, reflecting a subtle yet important principle: Leadership is not reserved for a privileged few—it thrives everywhere, blooming in the fertile soils of everyday interactions.

As a keen observer of leadership in various facets of human life, I consider myself fortunate to have witnessed the intricate interactions between differing leadership styles. This experience has painted a clear picture of many situations where contrasting forms of leadership are not only beneficial, but implicitly crucial, to effectively meet and manage the demands presented.

Military contexts, for instance, usually demand a more direct, authoritative approach to leadership. This isn't arbitrary, rather it stems from the very nature and demands of military environments. High stakes, high pressure, and the presence of immediate dangers necessitate an unyielding command structure.

In these circumstances, the need for rapid decision-making and instantaneous adherence to given orders is paramount. A rigid hierarchical structure evolves into an elemental entity which sets the cornerstone for the safety and outcomes of military endeavors. In such contexts, the prevailing form of leadership is marked by commanding presence, clear enforcement of the chain of command, and an almost unquestioning submission to authority.

On the contrary, environments that thrive under servant or participative leadership are replete throughout our sociocultural landscapes. Servant Leadership, marked by empathetic understanding and nurturing individuals' personal and professional growth, tends to find its stronghold in sectors like education, healthcare, and social services.

These are domains where an understanding of individual experiences and shared emotional narratives play a significant role. In such fields, the leader's effectiveness and success are innately linked with the growth, holistic well-being, and continual development of those they are entrusted to lead.

Participative leadership, another significant style, excels in environments necessitating collaboration, innovation, and collective decision-making. Ideal examples of such contexts can be identified in creative industries such as advertising, design, and technological development.

In these spaces, leaders empower employees to contribute their ideas and take part in organizational decision-making processes. This collective wisdom garnered fosters improved employee morale, solidifies their intrinsic drive since they possess a shared ownership of goals and outcomes, and catapults the organization towards unprecedented heights.

The ability to recognize and distinguish between these divergent environments is an indispensable skill for effective leadership. Leaders who aspire to strike a harmonious balance in their approach must comprehend the necessities and demands of each situation. Adapting one's leadership style to meet these requirements can often be the singular line that differentiates an effective leader from an ineffective one.

At the heart of the narrative that we delve into — "Unseen Leadership" — it is paramount to clarify that we do not negate or invalidate other forms of leadership. On the contrary, this narrative is a recognition of the diverse topology of human experiences where differing leadership styles meet.

This narrative primarily serves as a poignant reminder that we all contain within us the inherent capacity to lead in our everyday life. This form of leadership may not always corrclate with widcly recognized styles or approaches. Nevertheless, its influence and impact are no less significant.

In essence, the main objective of this narrative is to internalize the understanding that regardless of our environmental constraints, each of us possesses the potential to exercise meaningful leadership. The task at hand is to discern the surrounding subtleties and match our leadership style accordingly.

This harmony between conventional and unconventional approaches to leadership allows us to understand that no one style is superior to another. Each has its own time and place where it plays a dominant role. By striving to recognize and adapt these styles according to our environments, we can contribute richly to the collective experiences that surround us and simultaneously awaken our 'Unseen Leadership' potential.

Reflect on the earlier chapters of this book; think about the array of characters that graced these pages. Each one embodied leadership in their unique, often unassuming ways. Despite the differences in their environments, industries, and the challenges they faced, a common thread stitched their narratives together — the powerful exhibition of unseen leadership.

The story of Louise, the quiet and introverted librarian, provides an enduring message that leadership can emerge from the humblest of places, arising not necessarily from those who lead loud lives but also from individuals who radiate quiet determination. This story underscores the significant impact one person's passion and commitment can have on an entire community. The tale of Louise saving the Picnic Primary School library is a testament to the truth that nothing is insurmountable when one is driven by a sense of purpose and resilience, as well as a dedication to a cause that reaches beyond oneself. This narrative therefore encourages every reader to recognize and embrace their potential to effect meaningful change, regardless of their personality type or perceived societal norms, bringing to light the power and value of quiet leadership.

In the delightful story of Donnie, the empathetic barista, it is important to consider how genuine leadership can manifest itself in a myriad of ways, including through quiet acts of kindness, understanding, and unassuming guidance. Donnie embodies this uniquely refreshing style of leadership, illustrating that impactful leaders are not always found on the limelight or in grand gestures but may emerge from daily interactions over a shared cup of coffee. Donnie's compassionate demeanor and silent wisdom strike a note that resonates with each individual he encounters, celebrating the notion that true leadership is not simply about a bold presence or physical authority but stems from empathetic connections and humble acts of caring - a lesson to be cherished and emulated in our everyday lives.

The narrative of Nurse Trish and Arthur brings to light a critical reminder: the transformative power that compassionate caregiving can possess. In a world where we often prioritize organizational needs and overlook emotional well-being, Trish's empathetic approach argues convincingly for the equal importance of both. Through her role, Trish touched and enriched the lives she encountered, proving that our innate human ability to empathize, understand, and offer kindness should not be underestimated but celebrated heartily. Her story also imparts a crucial lesson that shared experiences and personal connections can serve as potent healing forces. Readily embedding these principles into our personal and professional lives has the potential to create profound and lasting change.

It is essential to remember that James serves as a profound symbol of leadership that is not measured by rank or status, but by the ability to inspire positive changes, cultivate mutual respect, and create a sense of shared responsibility amidst shared circumstances. His story distinctly illustrates that no matter what the environment —be it a night shift at a factory or a corner office in a skyscraper—leadership can be wielded by anyone, from anywhere. It manifests through empathy, humility, and through a respectful, yet powerful influence over others. The central character, James, exemplifies that leadership is not about dominating, but steering; not instructing, but inspiring; and it resides in actions that quietly make a profound difference.

Eugene's story underscores the profound potential that lies in caring for the well-being of others, particularly through dedication to safety—a vital aspect often sidelined. Demonstrating empathy and prioritizing safety redefines leadership, suggesting that it is less about wielding power from a place of authority and more about nurturing a harmonious and protective environment for all. Eugene's actions effected a paradigm shift in corporate attitudes toward worker safety and team spirit, thus proving that leadership can originate from anywhere, regardless of an individual's designated role or title. Rather than being defined by hierarchies, leadership can be epitomized by commitment, integrity, and a deep-seated care for others, which is capable of initiating transformative change.

Eddie's story manifests the importance of recognizing and seizing the opportunity for leadership within everyday interactions and situations, regardless of one's professional role. In essence, the takeaway is to understand that concern and care for others, alongside the ability to inspire through the simplest gestures - be it a heartfelt conversation or a commitment to excellence and positivity in all tasks - hold the potency to transform environments and lives. With honesty, empathy, and positivity, even the humblest of roles can become a channel for leading and inspiring others. By personifying kindness and uplifting others, we can create ripples of change that extend far beyond our immediate sphere, perpetuating an enduring legacy of humble leadership.

In light of Kristen's journey, what ignites reflection is the enduring power of integrity. This story is a compelling testament to the transformative impact of honesty, transparency, and professional ethics within an industry that is often overshadowed by dishonest practices. An essential point for every reader to absorb from this narration is that success, when deeply rooted in ethical conduct, is not transient but lasting. It solidifies trust, cultivates enduring relationships, and catalyzes significant positive changes across the board. The crux of this tale lies in affirming that upholding one's principles and ethics even when faced with challenges doesn't hinder success - it enhances it, and more importantly, initiates a collective move towards better practices.

In Jackson's journey, we see a powerful reminder that true leadership transcends the mere possession of a title or position, and instead hinges upon one's ability to authentically connect, inspire, and grow with their team.

While it can be easy to assume that authority comes as a natural byproduct of climbing the professional ladder, actually earning the respect and trust necessary to lead effectively requires unwavering commitment, self-awareness, and integrity. Jackson's transformation into a morally authoritative leader, who won the hearts and minds of his team through his actions rather than his directive power, serves to emphasize that the essence of leadership is a responsibility built upon trust, respect, and constancy in both personal and professional growth.

After traveling through unchartered paths of unseen leadership, you might wonder: how can I bring this subtle leadership to life? Whether you lead a multinational organization, a small local community, or participate in the daily operations of an organization, the answer is simpler than you would expect: Start small.

Begin slowly. You don't need a grand, disruptive plan. Instead, like the many characters you have met, allow your actions to carry the seeds of empathy and shared understanding. Infuse your day-to-day interactions with these traits and let these seeds germinate naturally, fostering an environment of shared responsibility and shared triumphs.

For those who are currently within leadership roles, show your team that they are not just cogs in a machine, but valued members of a journey of shared aspirations. Give them the freedom to think creatively and input into processes that directly affect their roles. When the team encounters obstacles, remember that encouraging words and a shared analytical perspective can foster better solutions than haste or panic. Cultivate a culture of shared responsibility and genuine camaraderie, creating an environment conducive to cooperation, innovation, and communal progress.

In the broad spectrum of professional roles, each individual's actions, decisions, and responses serve as significant elements that contribute to the overall dynamic and performance of a team. Leadership capacity is often on display in these actions and is keenly observed by others, shaping their perception about the leader. For example, when a newly appointed leader chooses to work collaboratively on a challenging task with a team member instead of delegating the task, this action reverberates respect and commitment throughout the team. This calculated act of camaraderie can significantly uplift perceptions of their leadership.

In another scenario, consider a leader who handles a team member's mistake empathetically rather than critically. This insightful act of understanding can create a significant shift within the team, inspiring an internal culture of empathy, learning, and resilience that further enhances the perception of the person's leadership skills. Additionally, consider the smile or the kind word from those in the humblest, yet most important, of roles. Each of these experiences underlines the ripple effects of our actions on teams and leadership perception, emphasizing the importance of leading by example and the power of observation. It can indeed shape an individual's transition from being a mere title holder, or non-title holder, to emerging as an effective, respectful, and much-admired leader.

As we gradually pull down the curtains on this narrative of unseen leadership, here is a thought to take away: you are a leader. You've related to these characters, their challenges and victories, their quiet moments of leadership, their brilliant flashes of inspiration. Within you resides an invisible touch— the touch that can inspire change, foster shared purpose, and create a transformative impact.

You may not awe large crowds with dynamic speeches, achieve recognition through newspaper headlines, or command applause with dramatically successful ventures. However, within your universe — however expansive or confined it may be — you have the potential to change narratives. You can inspire trust, instill hope, contribute to a collective purpose, and in doing so, manifest your unique flavor of leadership.

Leadership isn't a ceremonial wreath bestowed upon a select few on an elevated stage. It's a universal ability, surfacing in the most unexpected soils and thriving in the most inhospitable environments. As you journey on, it's essential to remember this: the most impactful exercise of leadership usually comes in the form of seemingly invisible everyday actions.

In the unique journey as an unassuming leader, remember to hold the reins of leadership with empathy, shared understanding, and collective responsibility. Let these values guide your decisions, interactions, and, eventually, your leadership narrative. Begin knitting your unique symphony of subtle leadership, which will ripple through the canvas of shared experiences, leaving an indelible impact.

Embrace your ability to lead. Let it radiate in your actions, resonate in your words. May your leadership narrative create ripples of change that flow into a river of collective transformation. Echoing the quiet yet impactful legacy of the many characters you have previously read, let your leadership anthem inspire others to do the same — to touch lives and stir up silent revolutions, woven within the fabric of everyday minutiae. May you paint the canvas of your world with the brilliant hues of effective and compassionate leadership.

ABOUT THE AUTHOR

Cody J. Comstock

Cody, a proud Veteran of the United States Marine Corps, has always been passionate about leadership and making a difference. In his professional life, Cody applies his deep understanding of leadership and resilience to solving complex problems in the Information Security field. He loves spending time with his family on their land, embracing the simplicity and beauty of nature. Inspired by historical epics and the Old West, Cody enjoys stories of adventure and grit, which he believes teach important life lessons. When he's not outdoors or with his family, you'll find Cody with his nose in a book, always looking to learn more about how to be a great leader from the past and the present. His life is a blend of serving, learning, and loving — each aspect enriching the other.

www.ingramcontent.com/pod-product-compliance
Lightning Source LLC
Chambersburg PA
CBHW071218090426
42736CB00014B/2878